cross-national issues relating to the early-childhood workforce. She was an editorial board member of *Early Years* from 1998–2006 and joined the editorial team in 2007.

Rod Parker-Rees is a Visiting Research Fellow at the Plymouth Institute of Education, University of Plymouth, UK, where he was formerly the coordinator of Early Childhood Studies. He has been a co-editor of *Early Years* since 1999. Once upon a time he was a nursery teacher in Bristol.

Digital Play and Technologies in the Early Years

Technologies are a pervasive feature of contemporary life for adults and children. However, young children's experiences with digital technologies are often the subject of polarised debate among parents, educators, policymakers and social commentators, particularly since the advent of tablets and smartphones changed access to the Internet and the nature of interactions with digital resources. Some are opposed to children's engagement with digital resources, concerned that the activities they afford are not developmentally appropriate, limit physical activity and restrict the development of social skills. Others welcome digital technologies which they see as offering new and enhanced ways of learning and sharing knowledge. Despite this level of popular and policy interest in young children's interactions with digital technologies our understanding of the influence of these technologies on playing and learning, and on the role of educators, has remained surprisingly limited.

The contributions to this book fill in the gaps of our existing understanding of the field. They focus on children and families from Australia to England to Estonia, the how and why of encounters with digital technologies, the nature of digital play and questions about practice and practitioners. The book raises critical questions and offers new understandings and theoretical insights around one of the 'hot topics' in early-years research.

This book was originally published as a special issue of the *Early Years* journal.

Christine Stephen researches children's learning in the early years and the ways in which this is supported in preschool settings and at home. She has co-directed a series of studies of young children's encounters with digital technology and has co-authored many journal articles and two books about growing up with new technologies. Her concern with the influence of culture and children's everyday experiences at home and in their educational settings is reflected in her research on their play and learning in a digital age.

Liz Brooker was an early-years teacher before returning to research and teach at London University Institute of Education, UK in 1996. Her work has frequently examined early transitions in children's lives, from home to nursery and through the subsequent phases of schooling. She was an editor of *Early Years* until 2017.

Pamela Oberhuemer is a Visiting Research Fellow at the State Institute of Early Childhood Research, Munich, Germany. Her main research and publication focus is on Early Childhood Education and Care (ECEC) systems in the European context, particularly on

Digital Play and Technologies in the Early Years

Edited by
Christine Stephen, Liz Brooker, Pamela Oberhuemer and Rod Parker-Rees

Routledge
Taylor & Francis Group
LONDON AND NEW YORK

First published 2019
by Routledge
2 Park Square, Milton Park, Abingdon, Oxon, OX14 4RN, UK

and by Routledge
52 Vanderbilt Avenue, New York, NY 10017

Routledge is an imprint of the Taylor & Francis Group, an informa business

British Library Cataloguing-in-Publication Data
A catalogue record for this book is available from the British Library

ISBN13: 978-0-367-00125-4

Typeset in Myriad Pro
by codeMantra

Publisher's Note
The publisher accepts responsibility for any inconsistencies that may have arisen during the conversion of this book from journal articles to book chapters, namely the possible inclusion of journal terminology.

Disclaimer
Every effort has been made to contact copyright holders for their permission to reprint material in this book. The publishers would be grateful to hear from any copyright holder who is not here acknowledged and will undertake to rectify any errors or omissions in future editions of this book.

MIX
Paper from responsible sources
FSC™ C013985
FSC www.fsc.org

Printed in the United Kingdom
by Henry Ling Limited

Contents

Citation Information vii
Notes on Contributors ix

Introduction 1
Christine Stephen

1 The role of parents and parental mediation on 0–3-year olds' digital play with smart devices: Estonian parents' attitudes and practices 5
Elyna Nevski and Andra Siibak

2 Digital play: a new classification 20
Jackie Marsh, Lydia Plowman, Dylan Yamada-Rice, Julia Bishop and Fiona Scott

3 Interlaced social worlds: exploring the use of social media in the kindergarten 32
Helen Knauf

4 An ecological exploration of young children's digital play: framing children's social experiences with technologies in early childhood 49
Lorna Arnott

5 Digital play as a means to develop children's literacy and power in the Swedish preschool 67
Leif Marklund and Elza Dunkels

6 Teachers' dispositions towards the role of digital devices in play-based pedagogy in early childhood education 83
Ioanna Palaiologou

7 Developing a measure to understand young children's Internet cognition and cyber-safety awareness: a pilot test 100
Susan Edwards, Andrea Nolan, Michael Henderson, Helen Skouteris, Ana Mantilla, Pamela Lambert and Jo Bird

Index 115

Citation Information

The chapters in this book were originally published in the journal *Early Years*, volume 36, issue 3 (September 2016). When citing this material, please use the original page numbering for each article, as follows:

Introduction
Introduction
Christine Stephen
Early Years, volume 36, issue 3 (September 2016) pp. 223–226

Chapter 1
The role of parents and parental mediation on 0–3-year olds' digital play with smart devices: Estonian parents' attitudes and practices
Elyna Nevski and Andra Siibak
Early Years, volume 36, issue 3 (September 2016) pp. 227–241

Chapter 2
Digital play: a new classification
Jackie Marsh, Lydia Plowman, Dylan Yamada-Rice, Julia Bishop and Fiona Scott
Early Years, volume 36, issue 3 (September 2016) pp. 242–253

Chapter 3
Interlaced social worlds: exploring the use of social media in the kindergarten
Helen Knauf
Early Years, volume 36, issue 3 (September 2016) pp. 254–270

Chapter 4
An ecological exploration of young children's digital play: framing children's social experiences with technologies in early childhood
Lorna Arnott
Early Years, volume 36, issue 3 (September 2016) pp. 271–288

Chapter 5

Digital play as a means to develop children's literacy and power in the Swedish preschool
Leif Marklund and Elza Dunkels
Early Years, volume 36, issue 3 (September 2016) pp. 289–304

Chapter 6

Teachers' dispositions towards the role of digital devices in play-based pedagogy in early childhood education
Ioanna Palaiologou
Early Years, volume 36, issue 3 (September 2016) pp. 305–321

Chapter 7

Developing a measure to understand young children's Internet cognition and cyber-safety awareness: a pilot test
Susan Edwards, Andrea Nolan, Michael Henderson, Helen Skouteris, Ana Mantilla, Pamela Lambert and Jo Bird
Early Years, volume 36, issue 3 (September 2016) pp. 322–335

Notes on Contributors

Lorna Arnott is a Lecturer in the School of Education at the University of Strathclyde, Glasgow, UK.

Jo Bird is a Lecturer in Early Childhood Education in the School of Education at the University of New England, Armidale, Australia.

Julia Bishop is a Research Associate in the School of Education at the University of Sheffield, UK.

Elza Dunkels is a Senior Lecturer and Associate Professor in the Department of Applied Educational Science at Umeå University, Sweden.

Susan Edwards is the Research Director of the Early Childhood Futures research concentration at the Learning Sciences Institute Australia, Brisbane City, Australia.

Michael Henderson is an Associate Professor in the Faculty of Education at Monash University, Melbourne, Australia.

Helen Knauf is a Professor in the Department of Social Work at the University of Applied Sciences, Fulda, Germany.

Pamela Lambert is a Training Facilitator in Early Years Education and Transition to School at Deakin University, Geelong, Australia.

Ana Mantilla is a Senior Research Associate and Research Manager for the Early Childhood Futures at the Learning Sciences Institute Australia, Faculty of Education and Arts, Australian Catholic University, Australia.

Leif Marklund is a Lecturer in the Department of Interactive Media and Learning at Umeå University, Sweden.

Jackie Marsh is a Professor of Education at the University of Sheffield, UK.

Elyna Nevski is a Lecturer in the School of Educational Sciences at Tallinn University, Estonia.

Andrea Nolan is a Professor of Early Childhood Education at Deakin University, Geelong, Australia.

Ioanna Palaiologou is the Director and Head of Children's Services at Canterbury Educational Services, UK.

Lydia Plowman is Professor of Education and Technology, College of Humanities & Social Science at the University of Edinburgh, UK.

Fiona Scott is a PhD Student in the School of Education at the University of Sheffield, UK.

Andra Siibak is a Professor in Media Studies and the Programme Director of the Institute of Social Studies at the University of Tartu, Estonia.

Helen Skouteris is the Monash Warwick Alliance Joint Professor of Healthcare Improvement and Implementation Science at Monash University, Melbourne, Australia.

Christine Stephen is an Honorary Research Fellow in the Faculty of Social Sciences at the University of Stirling, UK.

Dylan Yamada-Rice is a Senior Research Manager for Dubit, a company that focuses on research, strategy and digital for children's entertainment brands.

Introduction

Christine Stephen

In contemporary post-industrial communities, young children's encounters with digital technologies are increasingly considered to be a significant feature of their experiences at home and in their educational settings. In this context, this special edition of *Early Years,* dedicated to *Digital Play and Technologies in the Early Years,* is a welcome and timely contribution to the field. The term 'special edition' is an apt label for this focus on digital play and technologies. The level of interest that digital technologies generate is indeed special among research and practice areas in the early years. Contrast the attention in popular media, policy and practice guidance given to iPads, computers and mobile phones with writing about small world play resources, construction equipment or creative materials and activities.

Digital play and technologies generate strongly held and polarised positions among parents, practitioners, policy-makers and social commentators. For many, digital technologies offer the promise of new and enhanced ways of learning and sharing knowledge. Others are opposed to children's engagement with digital resources, fearing that they detract from more developmentally appropriate activities, are associated with restricted physical activity and underdeveloped social skills. Parents evaluate the opportunity for their children to engage with digital technologies positively and negatively. Some are persuaded of the value of a more 'natural' and certainly less technological childhood, while others see digital resources as a way to promote their child's educational and employment prospects. Policy-makers are keen to capitalise on the apparent potential for developing new skills and the enhanced knowledge capacity which investment in educational digital technologies seems to offer. Additionally, manufacturers and designers argue that their digital products can motivate hard to engage children and accelerate learning.

Nevertheless, despite the doubts expressed by some researchers and commentators and repeated in blogs and newspaper articles, even a brief period spent observing contemporary everyday life makes it clear that children are clearly exposed to parents using mobile phones, enjoy opportunities to take photographs and enthusiastically play with apps on phones and tablets passed to them by adults. A look at the shelves of a supermarket or toy shop will make it obvious that there is a very considerable market for screen-based and interactive toys and games for children from birth to teens. It is hard to resist Kalaš's (2010, 16) conclusion in his report for UNESCO that

> it is not necessary any more to prove that ICT matters in early childhood education. New digital technologies have entered every aspect of our reality, including families and the lives of young people.

This special edition of *Early Years* draws together research about this pervasive feature of contemporary life from the perspective of young children and those who care for and educate them. We need to know more about this special topic of digital play and technologies if we are to advance the debate about the benefits and threats of children's engagement with digital resources, even if a resolution of the conflicting claims seems unlikely in the short term. Of course, the contrast in perspectives is made more acute because of the interaction of views on new technology use with other 'bigger picture' positions about conceptions of an ideal childhood, moral panics about contemporary parental practices, valued forms of activity for young children, the impact of experience on neurological development and broader cultural and social expectations.

In the light of the level of popular and policy interest in children's interactions with digital technologies, the extent of published research seems surprisingly limited. Some writers draw conclusions for all children from studies of the activities of older children, failing to recognise the distinctiveness of the interests, competencies and ways of engaging that are characteristic of children in their early years. There is a growing body of literature about the technological activities of three- to five-year olds but it typically reports either on large-scale surveys of children's use of technologies or much smaller scale explorations, sometimes using before and after models of enquiry to measure specific outcomes. There is some growth in work that investigates pedagogy, the mixing of traditional and digital play and resources and the influence of the context in which technological activities occur. But there is more to understand and ample scope for methodological innovation and theoretical and conceptual developments. Attention to the technological experiences of children under three years of age is even more limited and writing in this area can be uncritical, with assertions of benefits not justified by reference to rigorous, supporting evidence.

From the perspective of a researcher, there are two particular aspects of the growing literature on empirical studies of young children's use of digital technologies that are puzzling. Firstly, the concern on both sides of the debate and research about the value of technological play seems to be with the relationship between engaging with digital media and development (whether positive or negative), rather than the kinds of play afforded or the ways in which digital resources are incorporated into family life and educational practices. The belief in the value of 'learning through play' has led to a burgeoning of attempts to validate 'playing with computer games' as therefore educational and playing with interactive toys as a way of accelerating development has become a familiar marketing device. But what notions of play, learning and education are asserted in these instances? Claims about play and educational value become blurred around technological resources and should challenge us to clarify our thinking about the ways in which we conceptualise play and learning and the relationship between the two in the early years.

The second striking aspect of much of the existing research and writing about the pros and cons of young children engaging with digital technologies is the focus on screen-based technologies in general and computers in particular – technologies where the user and resource are typically static and any activity is entirely virtual. Concentrating on computers seems to ignore the availability of many digital and interactive resources that are more likely to afford creativity and possibly adventure.

Research about children's encounters with new technologies and digital play happens in the context of rapid expansion in the reach and range of digital resources. The advent of tablets and smartphones is perhaps the most significant change in the resources available to young children. This technological advance has influenced resourcing in early years settings and made a difference to the accessibility of digital resources for play and learning for even the youngest children. Along with all these developments come claims of positive outcomes for learning and changes in the ways in which children and adults react to the technology and to each other when engaged with digital resources. Early years researchers are investigating the efficacy of particular apps and the ways in which they are used at home and in educational settings, but there remains scope to extend our thinking about these digital tools to the bigger question of the contribution of digital encounters to learning and play.

Of course it is not just the material features and interface characteristics of children's encounters with digital technologies that make a difference to their experiences. The social context of family life and peer groups and the educational context, influenced by policy and practice guidance and practitioners' perspectives, all impact on children's everyday experience of learning at home and in preschool settings. We have begun to tackle questions about pedagogy and explore methods which reflect this ecological framing of digital play and activities. A body of international evidence about the impact of practitioners' attitudes, personal engagement with digital technologies and opportunities for professional development is accumulating and has implications for other aspects of the early years field. For instance, it would be interesting to pose some of the questions raised about practice and pedagogy with digital technologies in the context of more traditional preschool activities such as water play or construction.

An inescapable feature of digital technology in the twenty-first century is innovation and change. The rapid pace of technological change means that parents and educators have not had the same experience of growing up with digital technologies as their children. Contemporary technologies and their applications for work, learning, communication and leisure are significantly different from those available when parents and practitioners were young. Practitioners making cautious progress towards digital competencies can be in awe of the apparent ease with which children 'pick up' these skills. Nevertheless, children do need adult support and guidance to have positive encounters with digital technologies and there are important questions still to be addressed about the nature of adult–child relationships, knowledge and learning in encounters with digital play and technologies.

The papers in this special edition have been selected because of the contribution they make to gaps in our existing understandings and the quality of the research activity in the field. Each of the papers tackles more than one 'issue' of course, reflecting the interconnected nature of children's experience of the world in which they are growing up. The papers are clearly located in the context of early years experiences across a range of national contexts, including Australia, England and Estonia. They focus on children, parents and practitioners, on the how and why of encounters with digital technologies, the nature of digital play and questions about practice and practitioners.

Elyna Nevski and Andra Siibak make a welcome contribution to the literature on the digital experiences of children from birth to three years old and advance our understanding of the nuances of parents' perspectives on and practices with very young children and smart technologies. The paper by Jackie Marsh and colleagues which follows is also concerned with children's everyday experiences at home. Its focus is on the nature of digital play. Employing a particular framework to characterise play, this paper extends our knowledge about the play potential of the apps with which children interact and contributes to our thinking about the nature of digital play and its relationship with play with traditional resources.

Helen Knauf's contribution moves us from digital encounters at home to integrating technology in a kindergarten class, exploring the opportunities for communication afforded by new technologies and the impact that these innovations in practice had for all participants in what she conceptualised as the social world of the setting. Knauf's paper raises questions about the reciprocal relationships between the material and the personal and between digital communities and the experiences of young children. Lorna Arnott's contribution employs a different conceptual framework to explore how children play with the digital technologies present in their educational setting. Adopting an ecological framework, Arnott demonstrates how it is necessary to take account of the affordances of technologies, the context of the playroom and the social behaviours of the children to understand their experience with digital technologies in the playroom.

Leif Marklund and Elza Dunkels report on an exploration of the discussions among practitioners about the ways in which digital play can develop children's literacy. Their study extended the existing evidence on computer activity and literacy development to the use of tablets. They examined the impact that the practitioners' perspective about their roles and responsibilities had on their practices and priorities for children's digital activities and the ways in which they evaluated the digital tools at their disposal. Like Marklund and Dunkels, Ioanna Palaiologou is interested in the personal and professional digital practices of early years practitioners. Her work also demonstrates that the affordances of digital technologies and practitioners' understandings of their role and appropriate practice can interact to create dissonance between the need to provide digital resources for learning and the desire to maintain a particular conception of play-based pedagogy.

The final paper in this special edition by Edwards and colleagues again relates to the early years educational setting but this contribution is concerned with the development of a tool which practitioners can employ to judge children's current understandings of the internet and cyber-safety and to plan educative interventions. As they report on the development of this tool, the researchers discuss the value of a sociocultural theoretical framework to underpin their exploration of children's thinking about the internet and the practices that they associate with Internet use. Here again we are offered glimpses of the gaps between the ways in which adults and children construe digital play and technologies.

Together these papers offer new understandings and point to theoretical insights but they also raise further questions and point to the need for more empirical work and conceptual endeavours if we are to go beyond the increasingly polarised and sterile debate 'for or against' children having opportunities for digital play and learning opportunities with digital technologies.

Reference

Kalaš, I. 2010. *Recognizing the Potential of ICT in Early Childhood Education*. Moscow: UNESCO Institute for Information Technologies in Education.

The role of parents and parental mediation on 0–3-year olds' digital play with smart devices: Estonian parents' attitudes and practices

Elyna Nevski and Andra Siibak

ABSTRACT

In this manuscript, we analyse the attitudes and practices of Estonian parents (N = 198) who allowed their 0–3-year olds to use smart devices. We aimed to discover if there was an interaction between parental use of smart technologies, parents' attitudes and the child's age that would predict young children's usage of smart devices. We also wanted to find out what kinds of devices are made available for 0–3-year olds, how frequently parents allow the child to use them, the activities children are engaged in on smart devices and which apps they use during their digital play. Parental mediation practices were also analysed. Our results provide evidence that parent screen time, parent attitudes and the child's age are all associated with touch screen use among infants and toddlers. Parents give three main reasons when rationalising their child's touch screen use, related to education, entertainment and behaviour regulation. Although parental mediation strategies are dependent on the age and gender of the child, the majority of parents combine different mediation strategies in order to fulfil their role as mediators of young children's digital play.

Introduction

In recent years, digital technology and smart devices in general, and smart phones and tablets in particular, have taken an important position in young children's mediaworlds (Kucirkova et al. 2014). In fact, recent studies indicate that infants and toddlers (0–3-year olds) have also started to make use of smart devices in order to entertain themselves, to play and to learn (Cristia and Seidl 2015; Holloway, Green, and Livingstone 2013; Marsh, Plowman et al. 2015; Rideout 2013). Despite the growing popularity of smart devices among the very young, scholars studying the topic have not yet reached agreement as to whether this is a positive or negative phenomenon. On the one hand, scholars claim that touch screen technology promotes play and creativity (Marsh 2010), that apps can support learning (Michael Cohen Group LLC 2011) and thus may have a positive educational impact on young children

(Kucirkova et al. 2014). For instance, Yelland (2015, 225) has claimed that 'playful explorations that encorporate new technologies enable young children to have multimodal experiences' which promote engagement and thereby also impact their self-confidence and autonomy. On the other hand, it has been pointed out that smart technologies may pose a threat to young children's imaginative play (Levin and Rosenquest 2001) and may impact brain development, cause attention problems (Courage and Setliff 2009) and all in all lead to 'irregular sleep patterns, behavioural issues, decreased academic performance, negative impact on socialization and language development' (cited in NAEYC 2012, 3). For all the above-mentioned reasons, the American Academy of Pediatrics (AAP) discourages any media use by children under two years of age (2011).

Regardless of their stance on the topic, many scholars (e.g. Marsh, Hannon et al. 2015; Neumann 2015; Sims and Colunga 2013; Yelland 2010) agree that in order to ensure a positive impact of technology on children's development, infants' and toddlers' smart device usage needs to be a guided activity. Furthermore, in order to 'support infants' and toddlers' playful explorations with smart devices an adult should mediate this activity so that it is articulated and represented by the children in the variety of modes' (Yelland and Gilbert 2012, 2). Hence, the role of parents and their various mediation strategies in guiding young children's digital device usage cannot be overestimated.

As the majority of studies so far have studied older children's usage of smart devices as well as parents' mediation strategies, there is still a lack of studies which analyse the digital play activities of 0–3-year olds. Although this age group has been part of the sample in several recent studies which have explored parental mediation strategies and young children's practices either on smart phones (Baek, Lee, and Kim 2013; Roy and Paradis 2015), tablets (Michael Cohen Group LLC 2011; Yelland, Gilbert, and Nicole 2014) or both (Kabali et al. 2015; Marsh. Hannon et al. 2015; Neumann 2015; Nikken and Schols 2015; Lauricella, Wartella, and Rideout 2015), infants' and toddlers' practices as well as their parents' mediation strategies have not been the main focus of these studies. Although some qualitative studies (Marsh, Hannon et al. 2015; Neumann 2015; Schlembach and Johnson 2014) have specifically explored 0–3-year olds' engagement with smart technologies and the guiding role of their parents in the process, there is still a gap in the literature. Furthermore, the majority of studies so far have been carried out in the English-speaking world, either in the USA (Kabali et al. 2015), in the UK (Crescenzi, Carey, and Price 2014; Marsh, Plowman et al. 2015) or Australia (Neumann 2015), and the topic has only rarely been explored in other countries (Cristia and Seidl 2015). To the knowledge of the authors, no relevant studies have been carried out in eastern European countries.

The present article investigates practices of Estonian 0–3-year olds on smart devices and parental mediation strategies ($N = 198$) used for guiding digital play. We aimed to study if there was an interaction between parental use of smart technologies, parents' attitudes and the child's age that would predict 0–3-year olds' use of smart devices. We set out to explore parents' own usage of smart technology as well as their justifications for making these devices available to infants and toddlers. We also wanted to find out what kind of digital devices are made available to 0–3-year olds; how frequently parents allow the child to use them; which activities children engage in on these devices; and the apps they use during their digital play. Furthermore, we analysed the mediation practices used by parents and how these were linked with young children's digital device usage.

We believe Estonia offers an interesting setting for exploring this topic for several reasons. Firstly, the term 'e-Estonia' is often used (Kotka, Vargas, and Korjus 2015) to describe Estonia's emergence as one of the most advanced e-societies in the world, a constantly switched-on and tech-savvy nation. Secondly, the above-mentioned traits have also been documented in academic studies which suggest that Estonia belongs to the group of countries which could be classified as 'higher use, higher risk', i.e. where higher levels of Internet usage go hand in hand with a higher likelihood of encountering online risks (Livingstone et al. 2011).

Since no previous systematic studies have been carried out in Estonia to investigate toddlers' use of touch screen technology and parental mediation on 0–3-year olds' digital play, this study can be viewed as a pilot study to provide the first insight on the topic.

Theoretical framework

Important others as role models

Two different theoretical perspectives can be used for explaining infants' and toddlers' use of smart devices. First of all, according to Bandura's (1977) social cognitive theory, learning and behaviour occur through observational learning. In other words, important others, i.e. parents, siblings and peers, can be viewed as role models for the young child. Therefore, when parents or siblings are using smart devices at home, infants and toddlers may start to mimic their activities and later also try these out on their own.

In addition to mimicking their parents' smart device use, parents' own attitudes regarding new technologies and their possible impact as well as parents' own usage practices may also 'set the stage for how the home media environment is created' (Lauricella, Wartella, and Rideout 2015, 11). The importance of different experiences, activities, roles and interactions of a developing person with their important others, i.e. an immediate microsystem, is also stressed in Bronfenbrenner's (1977) bio-ecological framework which characterises human development as a process of reciprocal interaction between a developing person and their environment. Thus, when following this approach, it can be argued that 'the family habitus (practices and culture)' has an impact on the young child's engagement with new technologies (McPake, Plowman, and Berch-Heyman 2008, 24).

In fact, empirical studies (Lauricella, Wartella, and Rideout 2015; Roy and Paradis 2015; Vinter 2013) also reveal that families shape young children's habits in their use of smart technologies through personal example. For instance, findings of Lauricella, Wartella, and Rideout (2015, 15) suggest that the child's age, parent attitudes and parent screen time 'play a dynamic and complex role in children's screen time with these technologies'. According to their findings, children of parents who are active tablet and smart phone users spend significantly more time using tablets and smart phones, compared to the children whose parents use these devices less often (ibid., 14).

Furthermore, empirical studies indicate that parents' attitudes about smart devices also influence how much time their young children spend with them. For instance, parents who believe it is important for their toddlers to be familiar with technology are also more likely to allow their child to use their smart phones (Roy and Paradis 2015) or 0–2-year olds of parents with more positive attitudes towards smartphones and tablets also spend more time with smart devices (Lauricella, Wartella, and Rideout 2015). However, parents are not aware (in most cases) of their children mirroring their behaviour and underestimate the risks of the use of technologies by their children (Chaudron 2015).

Digital play practices of infants and toddlers

According to research findings, young children are spending more time using digital media than ever before (Chaudron 2015; Holloway, Green, and Livingstone 2013; Kotilainen 2011; Marsh, Hannon et al. 2015; Marsh, Plowman et al. 2015; Rideout 2013; Suoninen 2013). However, the time spent on using smart devices is dependent on the age of the child. For instance, studies in the USA reveal that children under two spend on average close to an hour a day with screen media, whereas in the case of the 2–4-year olds, this time has already doubled. The findings of a more recent study from the UK (Marsh, Plowman et al. 2015, 42) report that 25% of children under three years of age who live in a household which has tablets have extensive access to these devices.

On the one hand, the growing popularity of smart devices in this age group is often explained by effective marketing strategies which emphasise the educational power of these technologies and provide the children with 'a good start for learning' (Yelland 2007, 53). On the other hand, several authors (Else 2009; Michael Cohen Group LLC 2011) consider that the fun interaction these new technologies provide is one of the key factors for their success.

According to Yelland (2015, 225) 'new technologies have an important role to play in reconceptualising play in the twenty-first century', creating additional opportunities for young children's play by allowing them to play in multiple modes. Furthermore, it is argued that smart devices can influence young children's play in several ways, enabling children to 'make connections with many areas of learning and experience' (Broadhead, Howard, and Wood 2010, 12). For instance, Plowman and Stephen (2005) argue that touchable screens may help promote free play and rule play, but also stimulate young children's imaginative play and role-play (Plowman et al. 2012). In addition, virtual play may also include fantasy, socio-dramatic and ritualised play (Marsh 2010). However, as it is very difficult to isolate play from the wider repertoire of activities 0–3-year olds engage in on smart devices, we will refer to all the activities undertaken by infants and toddlers on touch screens as 'digital play'.

Baek, Lee, and Kim (2013) reveal that the educational aspect is often the main explanation parents offer to justify their toddlers' smart device usage. At the same time, analysis of the activities infants and toddlers engage in on smart devices indicates that young children mainly use these devices for entertainment, i.e. watching cartoons and videos, whereas use of educational content has been found to be relatively low (Baek, Lee, and Kim 2013).

Many parents make use of different applications to provide their children with additional educational opportunities. According to Goodwin and Highfield (2013), it is possible to classify these apps into three broad categories: instructive, manipulable and constructive. The former has elements of 'drill-and-practise' design as a homogenous response is required from the user; 'manipulable apps allow the user to manipulate elements enabling guided discovery and experimentation within a predetermined context or framework, whereas the latter allows users to create content and digital artefacts' (Goodwin and Highfield 2013, 380–381). Goodwin and Highfield (2013) emphasise that parents and educators need guidance in selecting the apps, and thereby also support in their role of mediators for their infants and toddlers because many of the apps have spurious content in spite of being classified as 'educational'.

Parental mediation during their child's digital play

Parental mediation is a broad term that includes both media usage restrictions (time spent with media and content restrictions) and strategies to prevent the potential negative effect of the media. It is generally linked with increasing positive effect of the media, helping children become critical media consumers and citizens (Linder and Werner 2012; Livingstone and Helsper 2008; Vinter citation 2013).

Livingstone et al. (2011) differentiate between four main parental mediation categories: (1) restrictive mediation, i.e. posting restrictions on time and content used; (2) active mediation, i.e. discussing the content, giving explanations or instructions; being present or nearby when the child is using the device; (3) technical mediation, i.e. using software of parental controls so as to regulate or block, filter or monitor child's activities; and (4) monitoring, i.e. checking the browser history after the child has used the device.

Previous studies have demonstrated that parents' use of mediation activities is dependent on the age and gender of the child (Nikken and Jansz 2014), as well as on parental attitudes and their own usage practices. For instance, parents who are concerned about the possible negative effects of using smart devices tend to apply time and content restrictions, whereas parents who believe in the positive effects tend to co-use the mediums or use active mediation strategies (ibid.)

Methods and data

Data collection

As young children's digital technology use has not been studied before in Estonia, we decided to use a quantitative approach and carry out an online survey in order to gain the first input about Estonian parents' attitudes and practices related to 0–3-year olds' smart devices usage.

We recruited the respondents through contacts with preschools as well as by launching a call on Facebook. First of all, we sent out an email about the study and its aims, together with a request to forward the link of the survey to potential respondents to all the preschool directors in Estonia. Preschools were asked to share the survey link among the families of 0–3-year olds. Then, the main author of the paper also shared the link on her own Facebook profile and in preschool communities and groups on Facebook.

A survey was compiled on Google Forms and distributed online in December 2014 (4 December 2014–31 December 2014). We decided to carry out an online survey in order to reach potential respondents who might not have been so easy to target by other means. For example, since it is possible in Estonia to take parental leave until a child reaches the age of three and many mothers make use of this opportunity (Biin et al. 2013), reaching these families through preschools' means only might not have been possible. Our analysis shows that 73% of the respondents came through a call forwarded by preschool directors and 27% through a call posted on a Facebook page.

Making use of an online survey does have its limitations. For instance, we were only able to potentially reach those parents who were able to access the Internet, but since almost 89% of Estonian households with children are connected to the Internet (Estonian Competition Authority 2013), we do not believe that Internet access was a major problem. Furthermore, as we set out to explore parental attitudes and practices related to digital technology use, we needed a sample that had access to the Internet.

A second possible disadvantage of an online study is potential unreliability of respondents because, unlike a face-to-face interview or a phone interview, we cannot be sure of the respondents' identity (Mukherji and Albon 2010). In addition, as we were able to study only the self-proclaimed views and practices of parents about their child's smart device usage, it is possible that respondents' self-presentations were inaccurate or were socially desirable responses (Paulhus and Vazire 2007).

Our online survey consisted of five parts. Following the questions from the 'Technobabies' study (O'Connor 2014), our first set of questions in the survey was related to young children's touch screen use. A total of 10 questions used 6-point Likert scales to ascertain what touch screen devices are available in homes (e.g. a smart phone, a tablet, an e-reader, a touchable mp3 player or some other), how often they are used by infants (1 – several times a day to 6 – never) and what kind of applications children use most often. Open-ended questions allowed respondents to add explanations.

The second part of the survey, relying on the study 'Zero to eight' (Rideout 2013), included 14 multiple-choice and open-ended questions about the parents' awareness, where and how often their children used touch screen devices, what restrictions they apply and what kind of content children are accessing. Questions focused on whether and under what conditions parents implement time and content restrictions, and whether the parents have received support and guidance for child touch screen use.

In the third part of the survey, eight questions (four multiple-choice and four open-ended) were used to determine the parents' attitudes concerning how touch screen use can affect child development. This part of the survey, however, is not part of the present paper.

The fourth part of the survey focused on parental mediation strategies and included questions about active and restrictive mediation and co-using. The respondents were asked to answer each question on a four-point scale, ranging from *1 – always* to *4 – never*. The active mediation scale consisted of four questions to measure parents' tendency to talk about media content while the child is engaging with the medium; the restrictive mediation scale consisted of seven questions to measure parents' tendency to set rules that restrict the use of the medium (restrictions on location, content and time spent); and the co-using scale consisted of three questions to measure parents' tendency to remain present while the child is engaged with the medium and share the experience without commenting on the content or its effects (Livingstone and Helsper 2008; Nikken and Jansz 2014, 2006).

We first tested the survey questions during a pilot study ($N = 7$) which helped us work out some procedural mistakes and eliminate misunderstandings in the wording of some of the questions. The pilot study was carried out in the course of one week and the participants were selected on a convenience sample basis.

Respondents

Our final sample consisted of 400 parents of 0–3-year olds, who expressed their attitudes regarding young children's usage of smart devices and their own mediation practices. We later divided the sample into two subsamples: parents who 'allow' their children to use smart devices – 49.5% from the initial sample – and parents who 'do not allow' their 0–3-year olds to use smart devices – 50.5% from the initial sample. In the context of this paper, we only study the responses of parents who allow their infants and toddlers to use smart technologies ($N = 198$).

The majority of respondents (88.9%) to our survey were mothers or female guardians of children and only 11.1% were fathers or male guardians of children. The greater number of responses from mothers is explained by the fact that, in Estonia, fathers tend to take parental leave less often in comparison to mothers and thus tend to spend less time with very young children (Biin et al. 2013). Furthermore, the domination of mothers as respondents to our survey can also be explained by the fact that, similar to other post-socialist countries, Estonian fathers are quite inactive (18%) among the parents most involved in children's Internet use (Talves and Kalmus 2015).

We obtained data about 198 children, of whom 53% were girls and 47% boys. Most of the data (29.8%) were collected on children aged 31–36 months.

The average age of parents responding to our survey was 32 years (respondents' age 20 to 50). The majority (63.6%) lived in the three largest counties of Estonia (Harju, Pärnu and Tartu), all of which also have the greatest number of preschools. The majority of respondents have higher education (68%), which refers to the fact that surveyed parents are mostly highly educated, live in urban areas and are rather young, with 68.5% of them under age 35. Our findings also revealed that parents' sex, age and educational level had no effect on parental mediation strategies, or time and content limits set for children's smart device usage.

Data analysis

Data were analysed with SPSS 22.0 using frequencies and t-tests for comparison of mean differences. Summary characteristics were created on the basis of individual questions' arithmetic mean. A total of three summary characteristics were formed: 'parent's activity with device (frequency)', 'child's access to device' (frequency) and 'child's activity with device'. The summary characteristics were formed by compounding questions in the first part of the questionnaire (six-point Likert scale) and dividing the sum by five.

Based on parents' answers to an open-ended question, we used Goodwin and Highfields' (2013) classification of apps into three categories of pedagogical design with an aim to study what type of apps young children used. Following the specified age of the target users provided in the app description, we identified all named apps ($N = 26$) also by age.

Results

Smart device usage among 0–3-year olds

The findings of our study suggest that almost all our respondents (98%) have a smartphone and the majority (65.7%) also own a tablet, both of which are used either once a day (40.9%) or several times a day (19.2%), mainly for reading the news and e-books (40.9%). Smart devices were also often used weekly for work-related reasons (54%), but also for entertainment and fun, e.g. for watching movies or TV programmes (20.7%) or for playing games (19.7%).

The correlation analysis results indicate that there is a positive link between parent and child activity with the smart device ($r = 0.29$, $p < 0.05$). In other words, the more frequently a parent uses a smart device, the more frequently it is also used by the child.

The most commonly used smart devices among infants and toddlers are smartphones and tablets, both of which are used every day by 39.4 and 25.2% of the 0–3-year olds, respectively. However, children very rarely (30.8%) or never (46.5%) use more than one type of

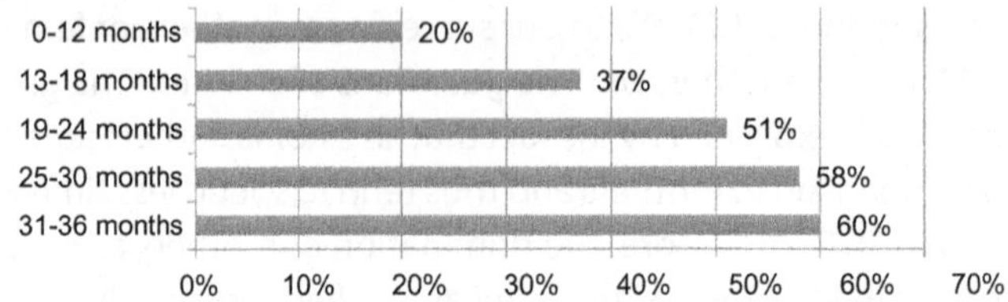

Figure 1. The age distribution of children (children who are allowed to use touch screens).

media at a time (e.g. play a handheld game while watching TV). Most often, young children use smart devices at home (96.5%) or in a car (28.8%).

The frequency of touch screen use among children increases with age (see Figure 1). The correlation analysis of touch screen guidance refers to the same tendency where the link between children's age and touch screen mediation is statistically significant ($r = 0.28$, $p < 0.05$), which shows that using parental mediation increases with children's age.

Many of the parents in our sample justified their young children's touch screen usage by emphasising the advantages and positive impact these technologies provide. First of all, the majority believed that children not only learn new skills (67.7%) but also acquire new knowledge (53%) while using touch screens. Secondly, many parents (55.1%) stressed the fun aspect of touch screens as they provide infants and toddlers with entertainment. Both of these justifications can be considered child-centred as parents had their child's best interests and development at heart. However, one parent-centred reason also dominated in these justifications: 67.2% of parents in our sample reported that they allow their child to use smart devices because these technologies helped occupy children while parents need to do something else, e.g. engage in household duties. Although, only 21.2% of the respondents claimed that they allow children to use touch screens because these devices also stimulate parent–child time together, the findings suggest that touch screen usage can be initiated by both sides, i.e. smart devices are used either upon the request of the child (44.4%) or when suggested by the parent (47%).

Digital play activities of infants and toddlers

The findings suggest that when using smart devices, infants and toddlers mainly (31.8%) watch videos, cartoons or TV programmes from YouTube, 'Masha and the Bear' being named as the main favourite of the children in the 0–3 age group. Parents' answers to the open-ended questions, however, revealed that with the help of parents, young children were also using smart devices to look at photos or communicate via Skype or Facetime.

More than half of the respondents (56%) had installed 5–9 applications in their smartphones, or tablet (28.8%), almost 40% from these applications were claimed to be installed with their young children in mind. The main reason (31.3%) for installing these applications according to the parents was the proclaimed educational benefits of these apps. Nevertheless, only 20% of the parents in our survey were able to name specific applications ($N = 26$) their toddlers actually used.

For instance, the parents in our sample named 'Talking Tom', which aims to shape empathy and compassion among young children, as one of the most popular applications among infants and toddlers. Yet, even in the case of 'Talking Tom', active parental mediation is advised as this application includes actions which can incite violence and may shape biased values (you can hurt the cat by pushing or striking his stomach). Several parents in our sample also mentioned the general apps of Toca Boca which are also included in the POSCON (Positive Online Content and Services for Children in Europe) repository. The popularity of Toca Boca is probably explained by the fact that the apps by this provider aim to stimulate young children's imagination and support their creativity in a non-competitive digital environment, coupled with a child-friendly usability. The analysis of the applications parents named as the apps used by their 0–3-year olds, however, suggests that the majority are not age-appropriate. Although many of the apps are not age specified by designers, only a few (Animal Numbers for Kids, Duckie Deck) were designed for toddlers, whereas the majority were designed for children who are over four years of age. Furthermore, our analysis of apps according to the pedagogic design used (see Table 1) reveals that the greatest number of applications can be categorised as manipulable (14) and instructional (11). The least

Table 1. Classification of apps following Goodwin and Highfields' (2013) classification.

		Pedagogical design classification			
		Imposed representations; high cognitive offload	Imposed representations which can be manipulated; medium cognitive offload	Student-generated representations; low cognitive offload	Specified age of the target user from the App description
Nr	Name of the app	Instructive	Manipulable	Constructive	Age
1	ABC Turtle	*			4+, Made for Ages 5 and Under
2	Animal Numbers for Kids	*			Appropriate to toddlers 1–3
3	Animal Sounds for toddlers and Kids	*			4+, Made for Ages 5 and Under
4	Animal Memory	*			4+
5	Baby Piano	*			4+
6	Big Forest Puzzle	*			4+
7	Turtle Math	*			Made for Ages 5 and Under
8	Sound Touch Lite	*			4+
9	Busy Shapes	*			Kids 5 and under
10	Õpi värve	*			4+
11	Toddler Coloring Book	*			For toddler
12	Angry Birds		*		4+
13	Toca Boca general apps		*		4+, Made for Ages 5 and Under
14	Duckie Deck		*		2–5 years
15.	My Zoo		*		for toddlers
16	Pou		*		4+
17	Zoo Sounds		*		4+
18	My Baby		*		4+
19	Subway Surf		*		9+
20	Talking Tom		*		4+
21	Talking Bird		*		4+
22	Tony the Truck		*		1 between 4 years
23	Pettson's Inventions 2		*		4+
24	Lego Duplo		*		4+, Made for Ages 5 and Under
25	Minions		*		4+
26	Kids Doodle			*	4+

*apps placed in the category.

represented were constructive apps, from which only 'KidsDoodle' could be named as one example where users can create content and digital artefacts.

Parental mediation of young children's digital play

The majority of the parents in our sample combine different elements from various mediation strategies for guiding their infants and toddlers' smart device usage.

One of the most often used strategies among our respondents was supervision, with 58.1% of the parents always staying close during the child's digital play on a touch screen, and 52% always monitoring their child's gaming behaviour.

Another strategy that the majority of parents used was restrictive mediation. For instance, 56.6% of the respondents claimed to have implemented both time and content restrictions during child's digital play; and a smaller group restrict either the time (22.5%) or the content (6.6%). Many parents (59.6%) implementing restrictive mediation check the game's/application's appropriateness or read content descriptions (45.5%) to ensure that these are age-appropriate and suitable. The frequency analysis indicates that in comparison to boys, parents tend to limit both the viewing time as well as the allowed content more in case of girls: 79.3% vs. 20.7% and 63.1 and 36%, respectively.

Categorisation of respondents' open answers showed that content restrictions are implemented mainly for violent videos, cartoons and games, e.g. shooting games, which are not considered age-appropriate for very young children. However, parents also restrict children's use of documents, and limit certain activities like sending messages, making phone calls or pressing random buttons. Respondents' open answers about time limits showed that parents implement precise time limits ranging from 10 min to a few hours a day. Based on these open-ended responses, we can assume that in many instances, technical mediation is implied to set limits to both time and content 0–3-year olds can use. For instance, parents claimed to use different parental controls, e.g. requiring a password, restricting Internet access and disabling built-in apps, on the smart devices.

Nevertheless, some parents (14.1%) did not implement any restrictions on infants' and toddlers' digital play. Furthermore, 28.3% of the parents in our sample never checked a game's appropriateness and 21.2% never read content descriptions. Based on the open-ended answers, infants and toddlers were considered to be smart enough to find enjoyable content themselves.

The findings show that infants' and toddlers' smart device usage is more frequent in those families where parents limit the media content and viewing time, compared to children in families where no restrictions are imposed. The result of t-test showed that there was a significant difference between parents who limit the media content ($M = 4.82$; SD = 0.71) with parents who do not ($M = 4.58$; SD = 0.82). Children use smart devices more frequently in those families where parents limit media content, $t(196) = 2.1$; $p < 0.05$. *T*-test showed similar significant differences between parents who limit viewing time ($M = 4.78$; SD = 0.69) with parents who do not ($M = 4.52$; SD = 0.95), indicating that in the families where parents set viewing limits, children use smart devices more frequently, $t(196) = 2.1$; $p < 0.05$. Smaller mean value indicates a higher frequency of smart device.

Parents also used active mediation: 44.4% of parents always ask questions and talk to a child during the child's digital play, whereas 44.9% of the respondents often point child's attention to what the child does on the screen. Giving feedback or specific instructions to a child during digital play, however, is less common: 36.4 and 32.3%, respectively. Co-using the device with a child was also practised, with 39.9% of respondents claiming that a child often, though not always, sits on their lap during their digital play.

Discussion

The findings of our study support Bandura's (1977) social cognitive model and Bronfenbrenner's (1979) bio-ecological framework in suggesting that infants' and toddlers' touch screen usage is influenced by the practices of important others, especially parents. Hence, similar to the findings of Lauricella, Wartella, and Rideout (2015), our results also indicate that parents' smart device usage is associated with child time with touch screens: the more frequently parents use these devices, the more frequently they are also used by the child. The majority of respondents use smart phones and tablets daily and their active engagement with these technologies at home is reflected in the infants' and toddlers' practices: 39.4% of 0–3-year olds use smart phones and 25.2% tablets every day. Considering the above, raising the awareness of parents on the topic is crucial.

Our findings also showed that the age of the child influences children's smart device use: whereas only 20% of children under one year of age had been in touch with smart technologies, this percentage rose to 60 for children aged 31–36 months. Furthermore, parents' attitudes about touch screens also have an impact on infants' and toddlers' smart device usage. The majority of respondents believed that by making smart devices available to infants and toddlers, they enable their children to learn new skills (67.7%) and acquire new knowledge (53%), and also provide the child with opportunities for entertainment (55.1%). Hence, similar to the findings of several previous studies (Baek, Lee, and Kim 2013; Broadhead, Howard, and Wood 2010; Marsh, Plowman et al. 2015; Yelland 2007), our respondents emphasised the positive impact and educational power smart devices may have on young children, but stressed also the importance of the fun aspect these technologies provide (Else 2009; Michael Cohen Group LLC 2011).

The main activities infants and toddlers engage in on smart devices are associated with the fun aspect touch screens provide since touch screens are mainly used by infants and toddlers to watch cartoons and videos. Using smart devices for educational content, however, has been found to be relatively low (Baek, Lee, and Kim 2013). Our findings are no exception here. Although a number of parents had installed 'educational' applications on their smart phones and tablets, our analysis of the apps named by parents revealed not only that their educational potential was questionable (e.g. Talking Tom and Toca Boca general apps), but that in the majority of cases, these apps were actually designed for children over four years of age. In other words, their content may not be age-appropriate for young children and does not carry the functionality and full potential needed to be effective for this age group (Aziz 2013). According to Goodwin's and Highfield's (2013, 380–381) categories of pedagogical design, the apps named by the parents can be classified into three groups: instructive, manipulable and constructive. The unpopularity of constructive apps was expected and could be explained by the relative lack of skills and knowledge of infants and toddlers. The greatest number of apps installed by our respondents could be classified as instructional apps where children are able to master new knowledge through 'drill-and-practice'. Such a practice however cannot be considered educational and thus may indicate parents' lack of knowledge on what could be considered educational and age-appropriate for their 0–3-year olds.

At the same time, our findings suggest that many parents of 0–3-year olds take their role as mediators of child's digital play seriously as they tend to combine different mediation strategies. Although many respondents were engaged in different mediation activities during their child's digital play, the analysis of open-ended answers also revealed an alarming trend – there were parents in our sample who believed that 0–3-year olds are themselves smart enough to find enjoyable content from the apps installed on the smart device.

All of the above indicates that there are parents in Estonia who are themselves in need of guidance and information so as to be able to fulfil their roles as mediators of young children's digital play properly

Furthermore, similar to previous studies, our results also reveal that parental mediation is dependent on the age and gender of the child. For instance, our findings coincide with Nikken and Schols (2015) and suggest that parental mediation strategies are rather used by toddlers (2–3-year olds) than in case of infants (0–1-year olds). However, in contrast to the findings of Nikken and Jansz (2014), who have found that parents tend to set significantly more general rules for boys than for girls, our findings suggest that Estonian parents set time and content restrictions more often for girls than for boys. As findings about gendered parental mediation practices of older children's Internet use in Estonia reflect just the opposite stance (Talves and Kalmus 2015), additional studies are needed to gain more input on the topic. At the same time, considering that Estonia is known for low gender equality and high Internet use, it is evident that parental mediation strategies of Estonian parents do not depend purely on a child's gender but on a more complex interrelation of gender and children's and parent's socio-demographic characteristics and parent–child interactions (ibid).

Although we believe our findings provide interesting and novel input on the topic of smart device usage among 0–3-year olds, we acknowledge that the study has some limitations. First of all, one of the weaknesses of the study is its non-representative sample which does not allow us to make any generalisations about the findings. Secondly, our sample was rather small and homogenous and thus the findings may not correspond with the attitudes and practices of other parents of 0–3-year olds. Additionally, it is also possible that other variables that were not included in our study may influence touch screen use among infants and toddlers. Furthermore, we were only able to analyse parents' self-proclaimed views and practices which may not reflect their real-life practices.

Due to the fact that smart device usage among infants and toddlers is a relatively new phenomenon, additional studies on the topic are needed. In addition to using quantitative methods, future studies should also make more active use of qualitative methodology. For instance, in addition to conducting interviews with parents, it would also be important to carry out observations in order to analyse how the 0–3-year olds actually engage in digital play on smart devices.

Disclosure statement

No potential conflict of interest was reported by the authors.

References

(AAP) American Academy of Pediatrics. 2011. "Media Use by Children Younger than 2 Years." *Pediatrics* 128 (5): 1040–1045. doi:http://dx.doi.org/10.1542/peds.2011-1753.

Aziz, N. A. 2013. "Children's Interaction with Tablet Applications: Gestures and Interface Design." *International Journal of Computer and Information Technology* 2 (3): 447–450. http://citeseerx.ist.psu.edu/viewdoc/download?doi=10.1.1.404.1245&rep=rep1&type=pdfhttp://howlifeunfolds.com/app/uploads/2015/07/2015-Back-to-School-Report.pdf.

Baek, Y-M., J.-M. Lee, and K.-S. Kim. 2013. "Smart Phone Use Condition of Infants and Toddlers." *International Journal of Smart Home* 7 (6). 123–132. http://dx.doi.org/10.14257/ijsh.2013.7.6.12.

Bandura, A. 1977. *Social Learning Theory*. Englewood Cliffs, NJ: Prentice-Hall.

Biin, H., M. Karu, M. Masso, and V. Veldre. 2013. *Analysis of Estonian Parental Leave System*. Tallinn: Praxis Centre for Policy Studies. http://www.praxis.ee/wp-content/uploads/2014/03/2013-Vanemapuhkuste-susteem.pdf.

Broadhead, P., J. Howard, and E. Wood. 2010. *Play and Learning in the Early Years: From Research to Practice*. London: Sage.

Bronfenbrenner, U. 1977. "Toward an Experimental Ecology of Human Development." *American Psychologist* 32: 513–531.

Bronfenbrenner, U. 1979. *The Ecology of Human Development*. Cambridge, MA: Harvard University Press.

Chaudron, S. 2015. "Young Children (0–8) and Digital Technology." http://www.lse.ac.uk/media@lse/research/ToddlersAndTablets/RelevantPublications/Young-Children-(0-8)-and-Digital-Technology.pdf.

Courage, M. L., and A. E. Setliff. 2009. "Debating the Impact of Television and Video Material on Very Young Children: Attention, Learning, and the Developing Brain." *Child Development Perspectives* 3 (1): 72–78. http://onlinelibrary.wiley.com.libproxy.ucl.ac.uk/doi/10.1111/j.1750-8606.2008.00080.x/epdf.

Crescenzi, L., J. Carey, and S. Price. 2014. "The Role of Touch in Preschool Children's Learning Using IPad versus Paper Interaction." *Australian Journal of Language and Literacy* 37 (2): 86–95. http://eprints.ncrm.ac.uk/3372/1/Crescenzi_Jewitt_and_Price_2014_The_role_of_touch_in_preschool_ch's_learning_using_iPads_vs_Paper.pdf.

Cristia, A., and A. Seidl. 2015. "Parental Reports on Touch Screen Use in Early Childhood." *PLoS ONE* 10 (6): 1–20. doi:http://dx.doi.org/10.1371/journal.pone.0128338.

Else, P. 2009. *The Value of Play*. London: Continuum.

Estonian Competition Authority. 2013. *Aastaraamat 2013* [Yearbook 2013]. http://www.konkurentsiamet.ee/public/Aastaraamat/Aastaraamat_2013.pdf.

Goodwin, K., and K. Highfield. 2013. "Apps for Mathematics Learning: A Review of 'Educational' Apps from the ITunes App Store." In *Mathematics Education: Yesterday, Today and Tomorrow (Proceedings of the 36th Annual Conference of the Mathematics Education Research Group of Australasia)*, edited by V. Steinle, L. Ball, and C. Bardini, 378–385. Melbourne: Merga.

Holloway, D., L. Green, and S. Livingstone. 2013. "Zero to Eight. Young Children and Their Internet Use." London: LSE, EU Kids Online. http://eprints.lse.ac.uk/52630/1/Zero_to_eight.pdf.

Kabali, H. K., M. M. Irigoyen, R. Nunez-Davis, J. G. Budacki, S. H. Mohanty, K. P. Leister, and R. L. Bonner. 2015. "Exposure and Use of Mobile Media Devices by Young Children." *Pediatrics* 136 (6): 1044–1050. doi:http://dx.doi.org/10.1542/peds.2015-2151.

Kotilainen, S, ed. 2011. "Children's Media Barometer 2010: The Use of Media among 0–8-Year-Olds in Finland." Helsinki: Finnish Society on Media Education. http://www.mediakasvatus.fi/publications/ISBN978-952-99964-7-6.pdf.

Kotka, T., C. I. Vargas Alvarez del Castillo, and K. Korjus. 2015. *Estonian e-Residency: Redefining the Nation-State in the Digital Era*. http://www.politics.ox.ac.uk/materials/centres/cyber-studies/Working_Paper_No.3_Kotka_Vargas_Korjus.pdf.

Kucirkova, N., D. Messer, K. Sheehy, and C. F. Panadero. 2014. "Children's Engagement with Educational IPad Apps: Insights from a Spanish Classroom." *Computers & Education* 71: 175–184. doi:http://dx.doi.org/10.1016/j.compedu.2013.10.003.

Lauricella, A., E. Wartella, and V. J. Rideout. 2015. "Young Children's Screen Time: The Complex Role of Parent and Child Factors." *Journal of Applied Developmental Psychology* 36: 11–17. doi:http://dx.doi.org/10.1016/j.appdev.2014.12.001.0193-3973/.

Levin, D. E., and B. Rosenquest. 2001. "The Increasing Role of Electronic Toys in the Lives of Infants and Toddlers: Should We Be Concerned?" *Contemporary Issues in Early Childhood* 2 (2): 242–247. doi:http://dx.doi.org/10.2304/ciec.2001.2.2.9.

Linder, J. R., and N. E. Werner. 2012. "Relationally Aggressive Media Exposure and Children's Normative Beliefs: Does Parental Mediation Matter?." *Family Relations* 61 (3): 488–500. doi:http://dx.doi.org/10.1111/j.1741-3729.2012.00707.x.

Livingstone, S., L. Haddon, A. Görzig, and K. Olafsson. 2011. "Risks and Safety on the Internet: The Perspective of European Children: Full Findings and Policy Implications from the EU Kids Online Survey of 9-16 Year Olds and Their Parents in 25 Countries." http://eprints.lse.ac.uk/33731/.

Livingstone, S., and E. Helsper. 2008. "Parental Mediation and Children's Internet Use." *Journal of Broadcasting & Electronic Media* 52 (4): 581–599. doi:http://dx.doi.org/10.1080/08838150802437396.

Marsh, J. 2010. "Young Children's Play in Online Virtual Worlds." *Journal of Early Childhood Research* 8 (1): 23–39. doi:http://dx.doi.org/10.1177/1476718X09345406.

Marsh, J., P. Hannon, M. Lewis, and L. Ritchie. 2015. "Young Children's Initiation into Family Literacy Practices in the Digital Age." *Journal of Early Childhood Research* 1 (14): doi:http://dx.doi.org/10.1177/1476718X15582095.

Marsh, J., L. Plowman, D. Yamada-Rice, J. C. Bishop, J. Lahmar, F. Scott, A. Davenport, et al. 2015. "Exploring Play and Creativity in Pre-Schoolers' Use of Apps: Final Project Report." www.techandplay.org/reports/TAP_Final_Report.pdf.

McPake, S., J. Plowman, and S. Berch-Heyman. 2008. "Learning from the Children: Exploring Preschool Children's Encounters with ICT at Home." *Journal of Early Childhood Research* 6 (2): 99–117. doi:http://dx.doi.org/10.1177/1476718X08088673.

Michael Cohen Group LLC. 2011. "Young Children, Apps and IPad (Research Undertaken as Part of the Evaluation Activities of the US Department of Education Ready to Learn Program)." http://sociallyspeakingllc.com/my-mission-for-socially/free-pdfs/a_study_of_young_children.pdf.

Mukherji, P., and D. Albon. 2010. *Research Methods in Early Childhood: An Introductory Guide*. London: Sage.

NAEYC (National Association for the Education of Young Children). 2012. "Technology and Interactive Media as Tools in Early Childhood Programs Serving Children from Birth through Age 8." Washington, DC: Author. http://www.naeyc.org/files/naeyc/file/positions/PS_technology_WEB2.pdf.

Neumann, M. M. 2015. "Young Children and Screen Time: Creating a Mindful Approach to Digital Technology". *Australian Educational Computing*, 30 (2). http://journal.acce.edu.au/index.php/AEC/article/view/67.

Nikken, P., and J. Jansz. 2006. "Parental Mediation of Children's Videogame Playing: A Comparison of the Reports by Parents and Children." *Learning, Media and Technology* 31 (2): 181–202. doi:http://dx.doi.org/10.1080/17439880600756803.

Nikken, P., and J. Jansz. 2014. "Developing Scales to Measure Parental Mediation of Young Children's Internet Use." *Learning, Media and Technology* 39 (2): 250–266. doi:http://dx.doi.org/10.1080/17439884.2013.782038.

Nikken, P., and M. Schols. 2015. "How and Why Parents Guide the Media Use of Young Children." *Journal of Child and Family Studies* 24: 3423–3435. doi:http://dx.doi.org/10.1007/s10826-015-0144-4.

O'Connor, J. 2014. "The Technobabies Project 2014: How Do Your Babies and Toddlers Use Touchscreens?" http://blogs.bcu.ac.uk/views/2014/01/27/the-technobabies-project-how-do-your-babies-and-toddlers-use-touchscreens/.

Paulhus, D. L., and S. Vazire. 2007. "The Self-report Method". *Handbook of Research Methods in Personality Psychology*. 224–239. http://neuron4.psych.ubc.ca/~dpaulhus/research/SDR/downloads/CHAPTERS/2008%20Handbook%20Research%20Methods/paulhus-vazire%2007%20chap.pdf.

Plowman, L., and C. Stephen. 2005. "Children, Play and Computers in Pre-School Education." *British Journal of Educational Technology* 36 (2): 145–157. doi:http://dx.doi.org/10.1111/j.1467-8535.2012.01323.x.

Plowman, L., O. Stevenson, C. Stephen, and J. McPake. 2012. "Preschool Children's Learning with Technology at Home." *Computers & Education* 59: 30–37. doi:http://dx.doi.org/10.1016/j.compedu.2011.11.014.

Rideout, V. 2013. "Zero to Eight: Children's Media Use in America 2013." *A Common Sense Media Research Study*, October 28. https://www.commonsensemedia.org/research/zero-to-eight-childrens-media-use-in-america-2013.

Roy, R., and G. Paradis. 2015. "Smartphone Use in the Daily Interactions between Parents and Young Children." *Psychology & Child Development Department CSU Stanislaus*. https://www.csustan.edu/sites/default/files/groups/Child%20Development/srcd_poster_2015_-smartphones.pdf.

Schlembach, S., and M. L. Johnson. 2014. "Parents' Beliefs, Attitudes and Behaviors concerning Their Young Children's Screen Media Use." *Dialog* 17 (2): 95–104. https://etd.ohiolink.edu/ap/10?0::NO:10:P10_ACCESSION_NUM:ucin1337363793.

Sims, C. E., and E. Colunga. 2013. "Parent-Child Screen Media Co-Viewing: Influences on Toddlers' Word Learning and Retention." In *Proceedings of the 35th Annual Conference of the Cognitive Science Society 1324–1329*, edited by M. Knauff, M. Pauen, N. Sebanz, and I. Wachsmuth, Austin, TX: Cognitive Science Society. http://psych.colorado.edu/~holtpatr/Pubs/SimsColungaCogSci2013.pdf.

Suoninen, A. 2013. "Children's Media Barometer 2013: Media Uses of 0–8 Year-Old Children and Changes in Media Uses since 2010." *Helsinki: Finnish Youth Research Network*. http://www.nuorisotutkimusseura.fi/julkaisuja/childrens_media_barometer_2013.pdf.

Talves, K., and Kalmus, V. 2015. "Gendered Mediation of Children's Internet Use: A Keyhole for Looking into Changing Socialization Practices." *Cyberpsychology: Journal of Psychosocial Research on Cyberspace* 9 (1), article 1. doi:http://dx.doi.org/10.5817/CP2015-1-4.

Vinter, K. 2013. "Social Mediation of Digital Screen Media Consumption among 5-7 Year Old Estonian Children: A Pedagogical View." PhD diss., Tallinn University.http://e-ait.tlulib.ee/318/1/vinter_kristi.pdf.

Yelland, N. J. 2007. *Shift to the Future: Rethinking Learning with New Technologies in Education*. New York: Routledge.

Yelland, N. J. 2010. "New Technologies, Playful Experiences, and Multimodal Learning." In High Tech Tots: Childhood in a Digital World, edited by I. R. Berson and M. J. Berson, 5–22. Charlotte, NC: Information Age.

Yelland, N. J. 2015. "Playful Explorations and New Technologies". Chap. 19 in *The Excellence of Play*. Maidenhead: Open University Press.

Yelland, N., and C. Gilbert. 2012. "iPlay, iLearn, iGrow." IBM Report. http://www.ipadsforeducation.vic.edu.au/userfiles/files/IBM%20Report%20iPlay,%20iLearn%20%26%20iGrow.pdf.

Yelland, N. J., C. Gilbert, and T. Nicole. 2014. "iPlay, iLearn, iGrow: Using IPads in a Play-Based Kindergarten Program." *Every Child* 20 (3): 1–203.

OPEN ACCESS

Digital play: a new classification

Jackie Marsh, Lydia Plowman, Dylan Yamada-Rice, Julia Bishop and Fiona Scott

ABSTRACT

This paper draws on an ESRC-funded study of play and creativity in preschool-aged children's use of apps in the UK. The main objectives of the study were to collect information about access to and use of apps in the home, establish the most popular apps and identify the features of those apps that are successful in promoting play and creativity. A mixed-method approach was used to collect data, including video filming of children using the most popular apps. In identifying play types that emerged in the analysis of data, the team utilised an established taxonomy, which outlines sixteen play types. This taxonomy was reviewed and adapted to analyse data from the project relating to digital play. Through this process, an additional type of play, transgressive play, was identified and added to the taxonomy. The paper outlines the implications of the revised taxonomy for future studies of play.

Introduction

It is becoming increasingly clear that the nature of play in the digital age is changing in terms of the resources available for play and the ways in which those resources are deployed in different types of play (Bird and Edwards 2015; Herr-Stephenson et al. 2013; Marsh and Bishop 2014; Stephen and Plowman 2014). Given the changes that have taken place in this area, tools that have been used by researchers to categorise play in previous studies may need reconsideration. In this paper, we revisit a taxonomy of play developed by the playworker Bob Hughes (2002) and revise the definitions of play offered in the light of technological transformations in the digital age. The revised taxonomy informed data analysis in a study of how far apps can foster young children's play and creativity (Marsh et al. 2015). In the first section of the paper, the key transformations that have taken place during the period since Hughes' taxonomy was developed are outlined, in order to provide a context for the study. The research design and methodology of the study in which Hughes' adapted tool was deployed are summarised and the nature of the classification of play in the digital age is considered in relation to the specific aims and objectives of the study. In the final section of the paper, the revised taxonomy is discussed, drawing attention to the addition of a category of 'transgressive' play and suggesting that it is not so much the *types* of play that have changed as a result of new digital contexts as the *nature* of play. The paper focuses on the revision of the classifications of play and does not report on the full findings of the study. These are reported in Marsh et al. (2015).

The changing landscape of digital play

Hughes developed his taxonomy of play in the first decades of computer use by young children. At that time, there were few studies that considered the relation between technology and play and, therefore, it is of little surprise that Hughes' definitions did not consider this aspect of children's play. However, in the years since Hughes' original work, various changes have taken place which impact on this area of study.

First, contemporary children use technologies in different ways to children growing up in previous decades. There are few data that can throw light on preschool-aged children's access to technology in 2002, as the first large-scale study of this age group emerged in 2003, when Rideout, Vandewater, and Wartella (2003) detailed the findings from a telephone survey of 1065 families in the US. A few years later, a similar survey was conducted in the UK. Marsh et al. (2005) analysed the responses of 1852 parents who reported on their 0- to 6-year-olds' media use. These US and UK studies identified that young children were engaged in the use of a range of technologies, including TV, computers and laptops, electronic toys, radios and music players, console games and mobile telephones, and developed a range of skills and knowledge in this use. Usage differed in relation to social class, age and gender across different forms of media. The average screen use time was around two hours a day.

Children today have a wider range of technologies to use than previous generations, such as tablets and smartphones. However, it would seem that the time spent with screens for this young age group has not increased. Rideout (2013) identified that 0- to 8-year-old children in the US use screens for just less than two hours a day (1:55). Nonetheless, the type of screen use has changed. There is evidence, for example, that children are spending less time on console games as they play games on other platforms. In addition, more children are going online from home and are more likely to watch television on demand (Ofcom 2015). YouTube and other social media platforms have become a popular feature of young children's online practices in recent years (Chaudron et al. 2015; Marsh et al. 2015). Whilst there is still a paucity of studies of children aged under eight (but see Danby et al. 2013; Davidson et al. 2014; Verenikina and Kervin 2011), these data indicate that more children are accessing online content at an earlier age than was previously the case. This is particularly the case since the advent of the tablet, made popular through the launch of the iPad in 2010. The touch screen technology enables young children to engage with games, apps and websites in a relatively easy manner, although there needs to be caution expressed with regard to this assertion, given that not all children find touch screens easy to use and some apps are not intuitive (Merchant 2014).

A further aspect of contemporary play is the relation between online and offline spaces. There have been various developments in relation to the way in which toys and other artefacts are digitally mediated (Burke and Marsh 2013; Manches et al. 2015). This leads to communication and play that moves across physical and virtual domains and integrates material and immaterial practices (Burnett et al. 2014; Marsh 2014).

There has been a range of concerns expressed that the rise of technology has led in some way to diminished play (for a discussion of these concerns, see Marsh and Bishop 2014).

However, it is possible to draw on well-established early childhood principles in order to identify ways in which this is not the case. For example, Edwards (2011) cites Vygotsky's (1978) theories of play as a leading activity in cognitive and imaginative development in her work on digital play, and argues that contemporary digital cultures provide rich opportunities for the promotion of play that is rooted in children's everyday experiences. This is not, she suggests, an inferior form of play; rather, it sits alongside more traditional play activities and is important for creative development, an argument developed in her later work. In a study of children's technology use in ten families in Australia, Edwards (2013) contends that there is a need to reconsider the relationship between traditional play (e.g. construction play, pretend play) and 'converged play' in post-industrial times. By converged play, she refers to play that is related to children's popular cultural artefacts and texts, including digital media. Rather than viewing the two types of play as oppositional, Edwards argues that they are interrelated and that it is no longer appropriate to view traditional play as the highest quality form, given that converged play can also lead to imaginative play.

It was in this context that the 'Exploring play and creativity in preschool children's use of apps' project was developed. The project was developed as a response to the lack of research outlining how tablets and apps could support play, but also to provide evidence that could offer a challenge to some of the moral panics expressed in relation to technology and play. A brief outline of the project itself is provided in the next section of the paper.

The project: exploring play and creativity in preschool children's use of apps

The aims of the project were to identify UK children's (aged 0–5) use of apps and to examine how far the apps they used promoted play and creativity. The project was co-constructed between academic, school and children's media industry partners, involving the Universities of Sheffield and Edinburgh, Monteney Primary School in Sheffield, CBeebies (BBC's channel for preschool children), Dubit, a media research and development company, and Foundling Bird, a children's television production company. All members of the team were jointly responsible for identifying the research questions, developing research tools and analysing data.

The project had four distinct stages. In the first stage, in early 2015, an online survey was completed by 2000 UK parents of 0- to 5-year-olds who had access to a tablet. The survey asked parents about children's access to and use of tablets and apps. In the second stage of the study, case studies were undertaken of six children aged 0–5. An ethnographic methodology was employed, as used in previous studies of children's technology use in the home (Plowman 2015). Over four to six visits to each family, each visit lasting approximately two hours, parents and children were interviewed and children were videoed and photographed using apps by both the researcher and parents. The researcher recorded field notes during each visit. In addition, play and creativity tours were undertaken in the home, in which the places, spaces and resources used for all manifestations of play, including technological, were identified by children and recorded by the researcher and families through notes, drawings and photographs. Finally, three children recorded their own play through the use of a 'GoPro' chestcam.

The third stage of the study involved an analysis of young children's top ten favourite apps, which had been identified in the stage one survey, in addition to a selection of augmented reality apps. Twelve children aged between 3 and 5 participated in this stage of the study and were videoed using the apps, primarily on their own, in a school IT room, filmed by the researchers. Seventeen hours, 21 min and 48 s of video recording were analysed. In the final phase of the study, the apps themselves were scrutinised and a multimodal analysis undertaken of them.

As the project aimed to identify how far apps promoted play and creativity, a framework for analysis of the data was developed which related to the children's use of the apps, combined with both parental and child reports of their play. We needed to identify the types and range of play and creativity facilitated by the apps in order to describe the features that promoted these dimensions. Creativity was identified when children produced new and original content (such as drawings), in addition to the identification of creative thinking using Robson's (2014) classification. This uses observations as the basis of an 'Analysing Children's Creative Thinking' framework, providing three high-level categories of 'Exploration and Engagement', 'Involvement and Enjoyment' and 'Persistence', together with a further ten sub-categories. The video data were analysed using these two frameworks, aided by the use of the software package Scribd 4.2, which enables the labelling of events in recorded videos.

Ethical issues were addressed throughout the study, in line with the BERA Ethical Guidelines (2011). The notion of informed consent underpinned the approach to the research, with an understanding that for young children, assent must be judged through ongoing assessments of the child's body language in addition to other potential markers of discomfort (Dockett and Perry 2011). If children appeared to be tired, then the interviews/video recording schedules were adjusted accordingly. Each family was given £100 of vouchers and the tablets purchased for the study were given to the school in order to acknowledge the commitments made to the project.

Classifications of play

There have been many classifications of play that have emerged from a range of disciplines. Given the way in which play is differently defined across disciplines (Sutton-Smith 1997), it seemed important to consider typologies developed in a number of them. One of the most established classifications was developed by Hutt (1979), a British psychologist. She identified three broad categories of play: (i) epistemic play, which is exploratory play in which knowledge of things is acquired; (ii) ludic play, which is play that draws on past experiences and includes symbolic and fantasy play; and (iii) games with rules, including games of skill and chance. This is a very useful framework for considering play in its broadest terms but, for the purpose of the study outlined in this paper, it is not sufficiently finely grained. Instead, there was a need to use a classification framework that enabled the identification of different types of epistemic play, ludic play and games with rules.

In sociology, other categories have been developed. Caillois defined four types of play: (i) agon – games of competition; (ii) alea – games of chance; (iii) mimicry – play as simulation, role play; and (iv) ilinx – play as vertigo (a state of dizziness and disorder, as when children spin in a circle on the spot) (Caillois 2001, 12). He proposed that these four types of games or play may be placed on a continuum, at one end of which is spontaneous improvisation (Paidia) and, at the other, contrived rules (Ludus). This can be related back to Hutt's (1979) model, as she suggested a distinction between exploratory and imaginative play, and games with rules. Whilst this classification of play is of interest as it includes attention to improvised play in addition to play bound by rules, both of which can be applied to young children's digital play, it was also too broad for the purposes of this study.

The team considered typologies of play that had been developed in educational projects in order to identify those that might be relevant for this study. Broadhead (2003) developed a framework for analysing play known as the 'Social Play Continuum'. This outlines observable behaviours in four domains: associative, social, highly social and co-operative. The framework enables the analysis of play in social situations, with the associative domain relating to contexts in which children play alongside each other. As Broadhead (2006, 193) suggests, 'The Social Play Continuum offers insights into the physical manifestation of learning processes through related language, action and interaction and to progression as represented in the four domains of the Continuum'. It was not felt to be relevant to this study because Broadhead's framework is largely focused on social interaction and learning, which was not the focus for this study.

Moving beyond psychology, sociology and education, a framework that had been developed in an interdisciplinary project that included attention to technology was considered. Two of the members of the project team involved in the study discussed in this paper had been engaged in a previous project on playground play, in which Bishop and Curtis's (2001) taxonomy of play was adapted to provide a more detailed model than the framework offered by Hutt (1979) (see Willett et al. 2013). That classification of play was, in turn, based on the work of Opie and Opie (1959, 1969, 1985, 1997). The adoption of that tool was considered to be too broad, as it specified play with high verbal content, high verbal and/or musical content, high physical and high verbal and/or musical content, high physical content and high imaginative content. This, again, would not have provided a sufficiently fine-grained framework to analyse the data produced in this project.

The final taxonomy considered was Bird and Edward's (2015) 'Digital Play Framework', which appeared relevant to this study, given that it focuses on the impact of digital technologies on play. The 'Digital Play Framework' sets out behaviours in relation to epistemic (exploration, problem solving, skill acquisition) and ludic (symbolic, innovation) play. However, Bird and Edwards (2015, 1153) emphasise that this framework 'provides a summarised description of children learning to use technologies through play that teachers can use to observe and assess children's learning'. Given its focus on learning, it was not felt suitable to be applied in this study.

As we were not able to identify a suitable classification of play that took account of the digital, it was decided to adapt an already established framework. Hughes' (2002) taxonomy of play was originally devised in order to enable playworkers to identify the various types of play in which children were engaged. It was adopted for our project because it enables detailed categories of play to emerge but, as none of the definitions referred to technology, the team adapted the framework so that it could be applied to the data emerging from a study of play using tablets.

The revised framework

Table 1 outlines Hughes' taxonomy and provides revised descriptions for each type of play, although it is noteworthy that the adaptations for our project retain many of the same characteristics as the original definitions. These adaptations were developed following reflections by team members, based on findings from their extensive projects on young children's

Table 1. Play types: adapted from Hughes (2002).

Play Type	Hughes' definition	Adapted for this project
1. Symbolic play	Occurs when children use an object to stand for another object, e.g. a stick becomes a horse	Occurs when children use a virtual object to stand for another object, e.g. an avatar's shoe becomes a wand
2. Rough and tumble play	When children are in physical contact during play, but there is no violence. Energetic play	Virtual rough and tumble play occurs when avatars that represent users in a digital environment touch each other playfully, e.g. bumping each other
3. Socio-dramatic play	The enactment of real-life scenarios that are based on personal experiences, e.g. playing house, going shopping	The enactment of real-life scenarios in a digital environment that are based on personal experiences, e.g. playing house, going shopping. This could take place through play with avatars, or by imagining that an on-screen virtual character is involved in such play off-screen
4. Social play	Play during which rules for social interaction are constructed and employed	Play in a digital context during which rules for social interaction are constructed and employed
5. Creative play	Play that enables children to explore, develop ideas and make things	Play that enables children to explore, develop ideas and make things in a digital context
6. Communication play	Play using words, songs, rhymes, poetry, etc.	Play using words, songs, rhymes, poetry, etc. in a digital context. Can include text messages, multimodal communication and so on
7. Dramatic play	Play that dramatises events in which children have not directly participated, e.g. TV shows	Play in a digital context that dramatises events in which children have not directly participated, e.g. TV shows. This could take place through play with avatars, or in chat rooms, etc.
8. Locomotor play	Play which involves movement, e.g. chase, hide and seek	Virtual locomotor play involves movement in a digital context, e.g. child may play hide and seek with others in a virtual world
9. Deep play	Play in which children encounter risky experiences, or feel as though they have to fight for survival	Play in digital contexts in which children encounter risky experiences, or feel as though they have to fight for survival
10. Exploratory play	Play in which children explore objects, spaces, etc. through the senses in order to find out information, or explore possibilities	Play in a digital context in which children explore objects, spaces, etc. through the senses in order to find out information, or explore possibilities
11. Fantasy play	Play in which children can take on roles that would not occur in real life, e.g. be a superhero	Play in a digital context in which children can take on roles that would not occur in real life, e.g. be a superhero. This could be through the use of an avatar, but may also include taking on a character off-screen whilst they engage in on-screen activities in the fantasy scenario
12. Imaginative play	Play in which children pretend that things are otherwise	Play in a digital context in which children pretend that things are otherwise
13. Mastery play	Play in which children attempt to gain control of environments, e.g. building dens	Play in digital contexts in which children attempt to gain control of environments, e.g. creating a virtual world
14. Object play	Play in which children explore objects through touch and vision. They may play with the objects	Play in which children explore virtual objects through vision and touch through the screen or mouse. They may play with the virtual objects
15. Role play	Play in which children might take on a role beyond the personal or domestic roles associated with socio-dramatic play	Play in a digital context in which children might take on a role beyond the personal or domestic roles associated with socio-dramatic play. This could be through the use of an avatar, or they could take on a role themselves as they engage in on-screen activities
16. Recapitulative play	Play in which children might explore history, rituals and myths and play in ways that resonate with the activities of our human ancestors (lighting fires, building shelters and so on)	Play in a digital context in which children might explore history, rituals and myths and play in ways that resonate with the activities of our human ancestors (lighting fires, building shelters and so on)

Table 2. Simon plays 'Minecraft' App[a].

Number of turn	Vocalisation/ Speech	Action	Gaze	Gesture/facial expression	Posture, proxemics/ haptics
1.	N/A	Simon is creating a building in Minecraft. He continually taps the screen and with each tap, a paving slab appears. His avatar stands at the front of the 'patio' area	Simon looks at screen	Not possible to see because of camera angle	Simon is half-standing, half-kneeling on a stool as he bends over the iPad, which is placed on a table top
2.	N/A	Simon taps the bar at the bottom of the screen. This takes him to a menu of building objects	As above	As above	Simon pushes closer to the screen
3.	Simon says 'See'.		As above	As above	As above
4.	Simon says, 'I know what I can use. I can use ...'	Simon scrolls through the choice of building materials available He taps on a picture of a brick and goes back to his land, where he can use his chosen brick on his construction	As above	Concentrated look	Simon sits up as he speaks He bends down again to press the screen

play using digital technologies (e.g. Marsh 2010; Marsh and Bishop 2014; Plowman, Stephen, and McPake 2010) and then refined through initial analysis of the data.

The revised definitions were then tested against the video data of children engaging with tablet apps. They were found to be highly relevant to the data, as they enabled the various types of play to be identified in ways which would not have been possible using the original framework. This can be illustrated by the following examples from the data. The videos were transcribed multimodally using the framework developed by Taylor (2014), which enables the notation of vocalisation/speech, gaze, facial expression, haptics (touch) and proximity (spatial positions) in any communicative turn. This was considered an appropriate approach, given the multimodal nature of children's practices when using technology (Kress 2010). All three examples were filmed in the school IT classroom, and the children used the tablets individually. The researchers filmed children using 'over the shoulder' shots, which enabled the children's actions to be discerned. The only other person in the room during the video recording was the IT teacher.

Hughes defined mastery play as relating to occasions when children attempt to gain control of physical environments, such as building dens. However, there were numerous occasions on which children could be seen attempting to control a virtual environment. This was particularly the case when children used the 'Minecraft' app, as this allowed them to create a virtual world using blocks, as illustrated by 4-year-old Simon (see Table 2).

The play continued as Simon built his environment. Once his building was complete, he manipulated his avatar so that it ran over the terrain of the surrounding environment. In this play episode, Simon could be identified as attempting to gain mastery over his virtual environment in a similar way to play in a physical environment in that what is at stake is the appropriate and effective deployment of the resources to hand.

Imaginative play, in which children pretend that things are otherwise, was a common feature of digital play with apps. For example, 4-year-old Jennifer played with an augmented reality app, 'AR Flashcards'. This enabled children to hold a tablet over a physical card on

Table 3. Jennifer plays 'AR Flashcards' App[a].

Number of turn	Vocalisation/Speech	Action	Gaze	Gesture/facial expression	Posture, proxemics/haptics
1.	Jennifer says, 'Iguana'	Jennifer holds the tablet over the picture of the letter 'I' and the iguana. When the 3D picture of the iguana appears, she presses it and the narrator says the letter and the animal's name	Looks at screen	Not possible to see because of camera angle	Sits on a stool and holds the tablet over the top of a paper with the pictures on it
2.	Jennifer says, 'Oh-oh, oh-oh, oh-oh, back' Jennifer says. 'Oh no, it's run away!'	Jennifer holds the tablet and waves her hand just above the paper	As above	As above	As above

Table 4. April plays 'Temple Run' App[a].

Number of turn	Vocalisation/ Speech	Action	Gaze	Gesture/facial expression	Posture, proxemics/haptics
1.		April moves the avatar by flicking it with her finger repeatedly, so that it runs along a path. The avatar is chased by monkeys making threatening sounds. There is a fast-paced soundtrack, adding to the tension	April looks at the screen	Not possible to see because of camera angle	April is kneeling on the floor, with the tablet placed on a stool in front of her
2.	April says, 'Uh!', with an expression of surprise/shock	The avatar falls down a crack in the road			April moves back a little as she says this

which a letter of the alphabet and related animal were depicted and then a 3D representation of the animal would appear (see Table 3).

In this instance, Jennifer pretends the iguana has run away from the screen, thus imaginatively extending the limits of this app. There were many instances of imaginative play, such as when children treated digital pets as 'real' animals and pretended to care for them when using the 'Talking Tom' app.

Hughes identified deep play as play in which children encounter risky experiences, or feel as though they have to fight for survival. He offered examples that were based on children's interaction with the outdoor environment, but this type of play can also occur in a digital environment, as when 3-year-old April played the app 'Temple Run' (see Table 4).

April had previously played this game and stated that she found it scary, so it is of interest that she wanted to play it again. As numerous scholars have attested, humans are attracted to fearful, imaginary experiences (Clasen 2012; Tudor 1997). In this kind of digital play, children experience tension and fear as they do in risky offline play, but they have more control over the outcomes; it is relatively easy to switch a digital game off if it is causing too much emotional stress, whereas this is not always possible with deep play in a physical environment.

One aspect of play that could not be accounted for by Hughes' framework was transgressive play. This can occur in both digital and non-digital environments. In the study outlined in this paper, transgressive play occurred when children used features of the apps that were not part of the design, thus transgressing the app producers' intentions. This was the case in 3-year-old Arjun's play, when he was observed playing 'Alphablocks' on the CBeebies Playtime app. Rather than adhering to the game's rules by placing the alphabet blocks on the line underneath the depiction of a word he was supposed to spell, he raised the block up to the top of the screen and made it disappear, then released the block to bounce back on the screen as he said, 'Peek-a-boo!'. This example, in addition to other instances in the data from the study, suggests that 'transgressive play' needs to be added to the framework, with the following definition:

> Play in which children contest, resist and/or transgress expected norms, rules and perceived restrictions in both digital and non-digital contexts.

In the examples offered above, it can be seen that Hughes' framework could be applied to play within a digital context. With the revised definitions, the framework enabled a comprehensive analysis of the types of play which emerged from young children's play using apps on tablets.[1] All but two of Hughes' (2002) 16 play types were identified in children's play with apps across the school and homes. The two types of play not observed were 'Recapitulative play' and 'Rough and tumble' play. Rough and tumble play relates to physical contact, and whilst there are virtual replications of this in online play (see Marsh 2010), this was not observed in this study. Recapitulative play is a category of play that is difficult to discern as it often overlaps with other play types, and Hughes (2002) felt that it occurs primarily when children have access to nature, although it could be argued that recapitulative play did occur in this study when children were using the *Minecraft* app, as they built dens and created civilisations.

Conclusion

This study has indicated that Hughes' taxonomy can be applied in a digital context, albeit with appropriate adaptations. It has demonstrated that what changes in digital contexts is not so much the types of play possible, but the nature of that play. Contemporary play draws on both the digital and non-digital properties of things and in doing so moves fluidly across boundaries of space and time in ways that were not possible in the pre-digital era. The findings of this study provide a counterpoint to those who seek to dichotomise digital and non-digital play, suggesting that play with digital technologies is not 'real play' (Palmer 2016).

There are a number of implications of the findings of this project for future studies of play. First, the adaptation of Hughes' taxonomy provides a useful framework for analysing other instances of young children's play in digital contexts. With the proviso that Hughes' original framework should be extended with the addition of 'transgressive play', it can be viewed as a robust tool for this kind of analysis given that the adapted framework was extensively tested on over 17 h of video data.

Second, Hughes' revised taxonomy can be applied to the digital play of older children, young people and adults. This study was focused on children aged under five, but similar types of play can be found in studies with older children (Kafai and Giang 2008). It would be possible, and even desirable, to engage young people in critical reflections on their own play across digital and non-digital spaces in order that the definitions could be refined further and be built on participatory approaches to the development of analytical tools. This process of adaptation can be a two-way process of adaptation. Using the taxonomy in a digital context may highlight an additional form of play that has not been identified originally and is equally applicable in digital and non-digital contexts and vice versa.

Finally, it is contended that this study makes a significant contribution to the field of play studies, as it points to the way in which future analyses of play should pay attention to the way in which the dichotomies of online/offline, physical/virtual and material/shape the activities, and it provides a means of classifying play types in this context. Whilst we would suggest that the research on young children's digital play is very much work in progress, this paper offers a robust tool that can inform studies in the area in the years ahead, and can be refined and adapted further as the possibilities for additional changes in the play landscape grow in the light of technological changes in society.

Note

1. For further discussion of the findings from the study, see Marsh et al. (2015).

Disclosure statement

No potential conflict of interest was reported by the authors.

Funding

This work was funded by the Economic and Social Research Council [grant number ES/M006409/1].

ORCID

Jackie Marsh http://orcid.org/0000-0001-6192-6198
Lydia Plowman http://orcid.org/0000-0003-2068-6428

References

Bird, J., and S. Edwards. 2015. "Children Learning to Use Technologies through Play: A Digital Play Framework." *British Journal of Educational Technology* 46 (6): 1149–1160.

Bishop, J. C., and M. Curtis, eds. 2001. *Play Today in the Primary School Playground: Life, Learning and Creativity*. Buckingham: Open University Press.

Broadhead, P. 2003. *Early Years Play and Learning: Developing Social Skills and Cooperation*. London: RoutledgeFalmer.

Broadhead, P. 2006. "Developing an Understanding of Young Children's Learning through Play: The Place of Observation, Interaction and Reflection." *British Educational Research Journal* 32 (2): 191–207.

Burke, A., and J. Marsh, eds. 2013. *Children's Virtual Play Worlds: Culture, Learning and Participation*. New York: Peter Lang.

Burnett, C., G. Merchant, K. Pahl, and J. Rowsell. 2014. "The (Im)materiality of Literacy: The Significance of Subjectivity to New Literacies Research." *Discourse: Studies in the Cultural Politics of Education* 35 (1): 90–103.

Caillois, R. 2001. *Man, Play and Games*. Champaign: University of Illinois Press.

Chaudron, S., M. E. Beutel, M. Černikova, V. Donoso, M. Dreier, B. Fletcher-Watson, A.-S. Heikkilä, et al. 2015. *Young Children (0–8) and Digital Technology: A Qualitative Exploratory Study across Seven Countries*. Joint Research Centre, European Commission. http://publications.jrc.ec.europa.eu/repository/handle/JRC93239.

Clasen, M. 2012. "'Can't Sleep, Clowns Will Eat Me': Telling Scary Stories." In *Telling Stories: Literature and Evolution*, edited by C. Gansel and D. Vanderbeke, 338–360. Berlin: de Gruyter.

Danby, S., C. Davidson, M. Theobald, B. Scriven, C. Cobb-Moore, S. Houen, S. Grant, L. Given, and K. Thorpe. 2013. "Talk in Activity during Young Children's Use of Digital Technologies at Home." *Australian Journal of Communication* 40 (2): 83–99.

Davidson, C., S. Danby, L. Given, and K. Thorpe. 2014. "Talk about a YouTube Video in Preschool: The Mutual Production of Shared Understanding for Learning with Digital Technology." *Australasian Journal of Early Childhood* 39 (3): 76–83.

Dockett, S., and B. Perry. 2011. "Researching with Young Children: Seeking Assent." *Child Indicators Research* 4 (2): 231–247.

Edwards, S. 2011. "Lessons from 'a Really Useful Engine'™: Using Thomas the Tank Engine™ to Examine the Relationship between Play as a Leading Activity, Imagination and Reality in Children's Contemporary Play Worlds." *Cambridge Journal of Education* 41 (2): 195–210.

Edwards, S. 2013. "Post-industrial Play: Understanding the Relationship between Traditional and Converged Forms of Play in the Early Years." In *Children's Virtual Play Worlds: Culture, Learning and Participation*, edited by A. Burke and J. Marsh, 10–26. New York: Peter Lang.

Herr-Stephenson, B., M. Alper, E. Reilly, and H. Jenkins. 2013. *T is ForTransmedia: Learning through Transmedia Play*. Los Angeles, CA: USC Annenberg Innovation Lab and The Joan Ganz Cooney Center at Sesame Workshop.

Hughes, B. 2002. *A Playworker's Taxonomy of Play Types*. 2nd ed. London: PlayLink.

Hutt, C. 1979. "Play in the under 5s: Form, Development and Function." In *Modern Perspectives in the Psychiatry of Infancy*, edited by J. G. Howell, 94–141. The Hague: Bruner/Maazel.

Kafai, Y. B., and M. T. Giang. 2008. "Virtual Playgrounds: Children's Multi-User Virtual Environments for Playing and Learning with Science." In *Children's Learning in a Digital World*, edited by T. Willoughby and Eileen Woo, 196–217. Oxford: Blackwell.

Kress, G. 2010. *Multimodality: A Social Semiotic Approach to Contemporary Communication*. London: Routledge.

Manches, A., P. Duncan, L. Plowman, and S. Sabeti. 2015. "Three Questions about the Internet of Things and Children." *TechTrends* 59 (1): 76–83.

Marsh, J. 2010. "Young Children's Play in Online Virtual Worlds." *Journal of Early Childhood Research* 8 (1): 23–39.

Marsh, J. 2014. "Online and Offline Play." In *Children's Games in the New Media Age*, edited by A. Burn and C. Richards, 109–312. Cambridge: Ashgate.

Marsh, J., and J. C. Bishop. 2014. *Changing Play: Play, Media and Commercial Culture from the 1950s to the Present Day*. Maidenhead: Open University Press/McGrawHill.

Marsh, J., G. Brooks, J. Hughes, L. Ritchie, and S. Roberts. 2005. *Digital Beginnings: Young Children's Use of Popular Culture, Media and New Technologies*. Sheffield: University of Sheffield. www.digitalbeginnings.shef.ac.uk/DigitalBeginningsReport.pdf.

Marsh, J., L. Plowman, D. Yamada-Rice, J. C. Bishop, J. Lahmar, F. Scott, A. Davenport, et al. 2015. *Exploring Play and Creativity in Pre-Schoolers' Use of Apps: Final Project Report*. www.techandplay.org.

Merchant, G. 2014. "Apps, Adults and Young Children: Researching Digital Literacy Practices in Context." In *Discourse and Digital Practices: Doing Discourse Analysis in the Digital Age*, edited by R. Jones, A. Chik, and C. Hafner, 144–157. Oxford: Taylor & Francis.

Ofcom. 2015. *Children and Parents: Media Use and Attitudes Report*. London: Ofcom. http://stakeholders.ofcom.org.uk/market-data-research/other/research-publications/childrens/children-parents-nov-15/

Opie, I., and P. Opie. 1959. *The Lore and Language of Schoolchildren*. Oxford: Oxford University Press.

Opie, I., and P. Opie. 1969. *Children's Games in Street and Playground*. Oxford: Clarendon Press.

Opie, I., and P. Opie. 1985. *The Singing Game*. Oxford: Oxford University Press.

Opie, I., and P. Opie. 1997. *Children's Games with Things*. Oxford: Oxford University Press.

Palmer, S. 2016. "Why the IPad is a Far Bigger Threat to Our Children than Anyone Realises." *Daily Mail*, January 27, 2016. http://www.dailymail.co.uk/femail/article-3420064/Why-iPad-far-bigger-threat-children-realises-Ten-years-ago-psychologist-SUE-PALMER-predicted-toxic-effects-social-media-sees-worrying-new-danger.html.

Plowman, L. 2015. "Researching Young Children's Everyday Uses of Technology in the Family Home." *Interacting with Computers* 27 (1): 36–46.

Plowman, L., C. Stephen, and J. McPake. 2010. *Growing up with Technology: Young Children Learning in a Digital World*. London: Routledge.

Rideout, V. J. 2013. *Zero to Eight: Children's Media Use in America*. San Francisco, CA: Common Sense Media.

Rideout, V. J., E. A. Vandewater, and E. A. Wartella. 2003. *Zero to Six: Electronic Media in the Lives of Infants, Toddlers and Preschoolers*. Washington, DC: Kaiser Foundation.

Robson, S. 2014. "The Analysing Children's Creative Thinking Framework: Development of an Observation-Led Approach to Identifying and Analysing Young Children's Creative Thinking." *British Educational Research Journal* 40 (1): 121–134.

Stephen, C., and L. Plowman. 2014. "Digital Play." In *The SAGE Handbook of Play and Learning in Early Childhood*, edited by L. Brooker, M. Blaise, and S. Edwards, 330–341. London: Sage.

Sutton-Smith, B. 1997. *The Ambiguity of Play*. Cambridge, MA: Harvard University Press.

Taylor, R. 2014. "Meaning between, in and around Words, Gestures and Postures – Multimodal Meaning-Making in Children's Classroom Discourse." *Language and Education* 28 (5): 401–420.

Tudor, A. 1997. "Why Horror? The Peculiar Pleasures of a Popular Genre." *Cultural Studies* 11 (3): 443–463.

Verenikina, I., and L. Kervin. 2011. "IPads, Digital Play and Pre-Schoolers." *He Kupu* 2 (5): 4–19.

Vygotsky, L. 1978. *Mind in Society*. Translated by M. Cole. Cambridge, MA: Harvard University Press.

Willett, R., C. Richards, J. Marsh, A. Burn, and J. Bishop. 2013. *Children, Media and Playground Cultures*. Basingstoke: Palgrave Macmillan.

Interlaced social worlds: exploring the use of social media in the kindergarten

Helen Knauf

ABSTRACT
The study presented in this article examines mediatization processes in an American kindergarten. The kindergarten is considered as a social world in which forms of communication, as well as the identities of those involved (children, teachers, parents), evolve through the use of digital technologies. The relationships between the different stakeholders are intensified through increased exchange. The role of children in this exchange process undergoes a particularly significant shift, since they come to be seen as active learners. Such developments are only possible if the teacher is prepared to be transparent and to invest a great deal of time. Parents warmly welcome the inclusion of such technologies in the kindergarten classroom and the contribution they make to the children's learning and family life. Digital technologies, however, are not entirely free of exclusion mechanisms.

Introduction: the mediatization of education in early childhood environments

In recent years, digital technologies have come to play an increasingly important role in educational contexts. The literature on this development has focused on the contexts in which older children (beginning at age 9) use digital technology, whereas the use of the Internet, social networks, tablets, and smartphones in early childhood has rarely been considered. In the last five years, however, an increasing amount of research has been carried out into the role, risks, and potential uses of digital media in early childhood. Particular attention has been given to the various ways in which children's surroundings have come to be increasingly permeated by digital technology. It has been shown that the domestication of the Internet has increased rapidly during the last decade (Marsh et al. 2015; Mascheroni and Ólafsson 2015; Röser and Peil 2012; Scifo 2015). Research into children's digital media skills has shown that children are 'digitally fluent from a very young age' (Palaiologou 2016, 14). For young learners (under the age of 9) it would seem that there are many potential uses for digital tools – for example, in fostering emergent literacy (Beschorner and Hutchinson 2013). It has also been claimed that digital tools promote social learning, since children often use and talk about them together (Aufenanger 2015; Beschorner and Hutchinson 2013). The successful use of digital technology depends on their being appropriate for the developmental stage of the children in question, support being provided by the teacher, and the integration of technology into the curriculum (McManis and Gunnewig 2012).

At the same time, there is still a great deal of uncertainty over the value of digital technology for young children. Early age learning processes are characterized by their immediacy and the importance of sensory stimuli; digital technology, by contrast, delivers indirect and abstract experiences. It is therefore no surprise that many parents and teachers are still cautious about digital tools (Burnett and Daniels 2016; Plowman, McPake, and Stephen 2010) and recent research has shown that digital technologies are rarely used in the context of early childhood learning and education (Endepohls-Ulpe, Quaiser-Pohl, and Deckers 2016; European Commission 2015). Digital media usage in educational contexts is strongly influenced by prevailing attitudes and prejudices, and several studies have indicated a reluctance to use such media (Blackwell, Lauricella, and Wartella 2014; Yelland 2016). Aside from the critical view that is often taken of digital media, many early childhood classrooms also simply remain poorly equipped with tablets, computers, smart boards, and Internet access (Endepohls-Ulpe, Quaiser-Pohl, and Deckers 2016; Wartella et al. 2010).

Despite these reservations and obstacles, recent discussion has focused on how digital media can be integrated into institutional teaching with young children (Beschorner and Hutchinson 2013). Research conducted from a cultural studies perspective seeks to describe, analyze, and explain societal developments without judging or classifying those digital technologies aimed at children as either 'good' or 'bad'. Culture, in this context, can be characterized as the 'shared meanings' in a society (Hall 1997, 1). An important model within cultural studies is the 'circuit of culture,' which helps to explain the processes through which meaning (i.e. 'culture') is constructed. The circle consists of five interrelated operations: representation, identity-formation, production, consumption and regulation. There is a reciprocal relation between these different operations, which means, for example, that identity-formation is shaped by certain modes of regulation and representation. One important task in the examination of the role of digital technology in children's lives is thus to understand how meaning is made and shared and the role that children play in this process (Buckingham 2013).

Where the relation between (young) children and digital media is concerned, the concept of mediatization provides a useful theoretical framework for further analysis. It enables a deeper understanding of the ways in which meaning-making, interaction, communication, and identities change. Mediatization is to be understood as a metaprocess, like individualization or globalization, which embeds the development of digital technology within social and cultural change (Krotz 2015). As a metaprocess, mediatization is not primarily characterized by a quantitative increase in the use of media, but by changes in the forms taken by communication, social relationships, everyday life, and the identities of those concerned. It amounts to a comprehensive cultural change whereby culture is no longer simply communicated through media but itself comes to be shaped by media; culture therefore increasingly has to be understood as media culture (Krotz 2015, 444). This of course raises questions concerning how exactly communication and action are changed by media. Media is understood here as a form of technology that helps to communicate content and that at the same time is 'experienced and adopted' by the relevant actors (Krotz 2015, 445).

One important feature of this cultural studies approach is its recognition and analysis of social worlds. Social worlds are interlaced constructs of interaction, since every individual belongs to a multitude of different social worlds. Social worlds may differ greatly in terms of their size, their visibility, and their openness. The members of a given social world share common commitments and activities (Strauss 1978); the process of mediatization promotes the differentiation and advancement of these social worlds. On the basis of this theoretical background, the present article interprets the kindergarten class as a social world, and aims to examine the ways in which this world, along with its key actors (children, teacher, families), is shaped by digital media and in turn shapes digital media.

Methodology

The study presented here examines how digital media are employed in an early childhood setting, which is seen as a social world. It analyzes how the use of digital tools changes the communication between the relevant social actors, and their perceptions of their identities and of the relationships existing between them. In order to provide some answers to these questions, we adopted an explorative case study method (Yin 2009).

For the case study, the aim was to examine an early childhood setting that had extensive experience of using digital technologies and social media. The selection process involved several stages. The first step was to find kindergartens that were publicly visible – on Facebook, Twitter, and/or with their own blog. The search was conducted in both German and English.

The majority of the 30 facilities identified in this manner were in the USA and Canada. Here, kindergarten is attended by five- and six-year-olds. It officially constitutes the children's first school year, but the classes serve to prepare children for their school career.

The second step was then to look for particularly active and experienced classes: active with regard to the number of digital tools used, the frequency and continuity of use, and experience over a period of several years. The kindergarten class examined for this study makes extensive use of digital tools and social media.

The kindergarten class described here is situated in a small town of around 9000 inhabitants in Vermont/USA. It is part of a public elementary school. During the study period, 17 children attended the class. The socioeconomic status of the children was mixed; one family spoke another language at home. There were 12 boys and 5 girls in the class. The teacher was 55-years old and has 32 years of professional experience.

The digital tools used in class include basic equipment consisting of a computer and four tablets for the children, all of which have internet access. The class also has a Smart Board, which (among other things) allows the whole class to see and interact with the computer-based activities. Several online tools are part of the classroom activities:

- Social networks: Twitter, Facebook, Seesaw, Instagram
- Blogs: Kidblog
- Interactive online tools: Padlet, Google Forms
- Tools for simultaneous communication: Skype, Google Hangout
- Direct messaging: emails

In the following discussion, 'digital tools' will be used as a collective term for these instruments.

In line with the case study approach, various forms of data were gathered during the investigation. Qualitative interviews, document analyses and observations were used as research tools. All of the interviews took the form of semi-standardized interviews, which were conducted using an open interview guide in order to ensure that the most important points were covered (Flick 2014). Interviews were chosen because they are particularly suitable for reconstructing the subjective theories of the respondents. As semi-standardized interviews do not put forward any hypotheses, and are structured very openly, taking their lead from the respondents' views, they also match the exploratory nature of the study. The main data sources consisted of qualitative interviews conducted with the teacher and two of the children's parents. The teacher was interviewed several times, because of her key role as the initiator and most important organizer of the use of digital tools. Furthermore, her experience puts her in a position to describe and reflect on the developments that have taken place in recent years. Parents were interviewed as an important target group and also as actors in the use of digital tools. Since children in the US only attend kindergarten for one year, a relatively short period which limits the experience parents can gather, parents were chosen who not only had a child in the group at the time of the study, but had previously had older children in the same kindergarten. This made it possible to access a greater pool of experience. In addition, four children were also interviewed, who have been selected randomly. In order to support the verbal communication with these interviewees, pictures of the different digital tools were provided. The children were also encouraged to show the interviewers the tools that they used in the classroom (Clark 2010). All interviews were recorded and transcribed. The interpretation of data followed the rules of content analysis. During the analysis stage, relevant passages were selected and summarized (reduction), and subsequently classified according to categories developed on the basis of the material (reorganization) (Roulston 2010). Each category was built by a cluster of quotes referring to the same topic in order to identify key topics.

In addition, documents published on a range of digital channels (Twitter, Facebook, Kidblog, and Seesaw) were included in the study. While Twitter and Facebook are public, access to documents published on Kidblog and Seesaw is restricted. The documents were screened, graded, and categorized according to their content.

Lastly, the procedures in the kindergarten class were recorded by means of overt and participant observation. The observations were logged using a non-standardized data entry form, to allow the greatest possible openness to the situation (Flick 2014). In total, five hours of teaching were observed. Interactions with and references to the digital tools used in these situations were noted. The aim of the observations and the document analysis was to fill out the picture outlined by means of the interviews. In order to consolidate the different stages of the study, its key findings were identified through a final review of the data.

The research presented here is consistent with the Code of Ethics of the Deutsche Gesellschaft für Erziehungswissenschaft (DGfE). This includes respecting the personality rights of the individuals involved in the scientific study. The teacher, parents and children interviewed and observed in this study agreed to be part of the research. The documents involved were either public or the parents consented to their examination for the study. Prior to publication, these findings were submitted to and approved by the institution examined in the study.

At this point, it is important to note that this is a small-scale study. The findings presented in the following section are neither representative nor generalizable. However, they do allow us to show the mediatization of early childhood settings – a phenomenon that is still in its infancy – in greater depth, thus providing stimuli for further studies.

Figure 1. Post on Instagram.

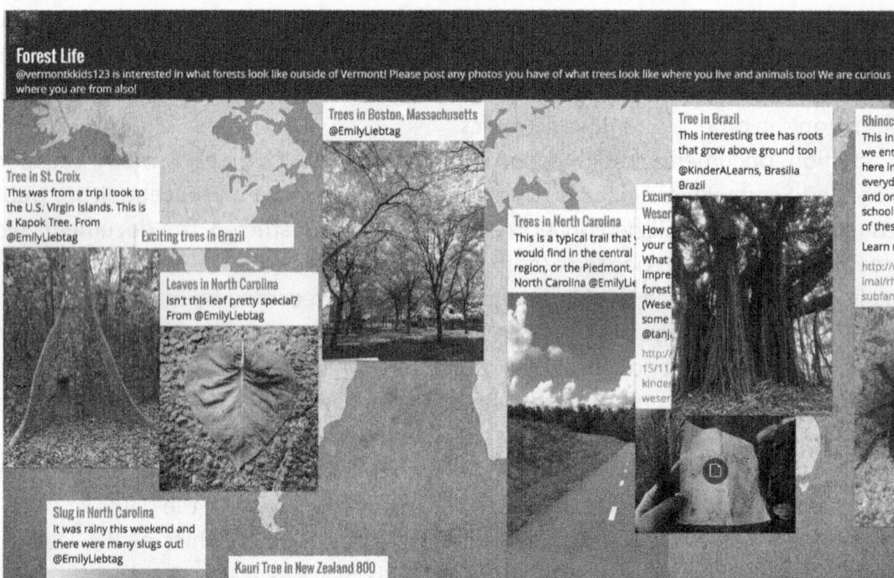

Figure 2. Padlet wall.

Results and discussion

The kindergarten class as a social world

Over the last seven years, the teacher has integrated various forms of digital media into her classes. The initial stimulus for this development came from an integration specialist in her school who drew S.'s attention to blogs. She subsequently came to employ an array of digital tools with her students.

Figure 3. A child's post on Seesaw.

Figure 4. Using Twitter in a class meeting.

Some of the tools are publicly accessible (e.g. Twitter) while others can only be accessed by a restricted audience – usually the children's parents (e.g. Seesaw). Typical posts provide information about visitors to the class, classroom activities (Figure 1, on Instagram), and field trips. Some invite other Twitter users to share their knowledge of a certain topic – for example by sharing pictures of trees or forests (Figure 2, on Padlet).

These posts seek to reach a global audience, while the contributions to the restricted platforms exhibit the children's own efforts (Figure 3, on Seesaw). These online tools offer different opportunities for documenting activities and gaining feedback.

All of these elements – aspects of both the on- and off-screen resources – contribute to making this class a social world. The formal frame delimiting the social world of the kindergarten class is clearly specified in advance and its members (children, teacher, families) and its site are likewise given. This world is thus well-defined and clearly differentiated from others. The central activity linking the members of this social world is education. The *raison-d'être* of the kindergarten is education; the children and the teacher come together in order to learn; and ideally parents are involved in and support these learning processes. This social world is small and its complexity is limited. Furthermore, it is tied to one place: it is in the classroom that students meet, talk to each other, accomplish tasks, give presentations, play, read, listen, sing, talk, and eat snacks together. Online tools extend this space into the virtual sphere. A Twitter account, for example, has been set up for the class, which provides information about its current activities. Using the class's internet access, the Twitter page is projected on to the wall using the Smart Board. This allows the children to formulate tweets together as a group, dictate the text to the teacher, and then post it on Twitter (Figure 4).

In this way, the social world of the kindergarten is connected to other social worlds and becomes visible within and as part of them (e.g. to people in the US or kindergarten-age children around the world). The responses to their posts by people from the 'outside world' allow the children to experience this connection for themselves. This is an important step towards collecting experiences from outside the 'bubble of a classroom' (Waller 2013, 138). Furthermore, a world map painted by the children is displayed in the classroom, allowing them to identify the physical location of their partners. This also makes visible the interlacing of different social worlds.

From an analytic viewpoint, the space of the real world is extended into the virtual sphere. This is why the location of the social world is bound up with the (analog and digital) technology used within it. The social world of this kindergarten class can be seen as undergoing a process of mediatization. During this process communication and interaction is transformed by the increasing use of digital technology. Rather than being a static world, it is continually under construction. The daily social media posts contribute to this construction process. In the following, the latter will be described from the perspective of the three sets of actors involved: the teacher, the children, and the parents.

The teacher's perspective

Changing intentions

When S. began to use digital media in her class, she did so in order to communicate with a rather small group of people: 'My initial audience was my parents, my families'. Her original intention was to contact families via a digital medium, which would replace the printed letters she had thus far sent them. Little by little, she began to integrate more interactive tools into her class. S. describes getting into Twitter as a personal breakthrough. This service enabled her to make contact with other teachers, from whom she received a great deal of encouragement and inspiration. S. became part of a network of teachers who shared their ideas and thinking on Twitter. S. then transferred her own experience to the classroom, opening up ways for her kindergarten pupils to communicate at the local, national, and international level. Recently she began using tools designed to share children's experiences and work in a protected forum (Kidblog, Seesaw).

This example of the adaption of digital media incorporates several aspects of a model, which identifies four stages in the use of digital media and is called the SAMR model because of the initial letters of the four levels: Substitution, Augmentation, Modification and Redefinition. While substitution and augmentation constitute ways of enhancing the primary task in question, modification and redefinition change the very nature of that task (Keane, Keane, and Blicblau 2014). When S. started writing her blog she only intended it to replace the printed letters (substitution); later, however, she added voting tools to the blog (augmentation). Through the use of social networks, new pedagogical objectives subsequently arose (redefinition); these have to do not only with the transmission of information, but also with (1) connecting with others, (2) supporting the development of digital literacy und (3) discussing the children's development with their parents.

Connecting with others. S. sees this form of connection as essential. For her, one of the main objectives of online activity is to enter into such exchanges. This, as she describes it, is the reason for using Skype or Google Hangouts to contact other kindergarten classes in the US or around the world. The world map mentioned above, which is displayed in a central position in the classroom, gives the locations of the people contacted most frequently by the kindergarten. For the teacher, the interlacing of different social worlds seems to be an important and explicit educational objective.

Digital literacy. Connecting with others is also part of an attempt to improve digital literacy. Here, emphasis is placed on internet safety. The school's motto, 'Be safe, be kind, be responsible,' is thus applied to online behavior. S. continually comes back to the ways in which one can protect one's privacy – for example, by learning how to log out of online platforms or deciding what content is appropriate to share on them, as the following example shows:

> One time a child said: 'Oh, can we tweet my mom? I want to tell her that I love her.' And I said: 'That's really great, so do you think, remember when we're tweeting we're sharing with the whole world, is that something that you think everyone in the world might be interested in?' and she said: 'No, probably just my mom' and I said 'Yeah. So when you see her, you share that with her face to face. And we save all our tweets to share with her what we're experiencing in the classroom and what we're doing here.' And really the kids understand that right away, that's pretty phenomenal to me.

In S.'s eyes, using an iPad or navigating an online platform are tasks that a child can easily accomplish. This is why, for her, digital literacy is less a question of technical competence than of the considered use of the relevant tools. This ties in with findings from Danby et al. (2016), who were able to show that pedagogical interaction and 'moral work' play a more important role than the technical side of dealing with devices, particularly in work with young children.

Involving parents. For S., the children's parents also have an important contribution to make. Her aim is to involve them in the children's learning, even during the kindergarten day. This objective matches with the model of interlaced social worlds, because by connecting with people outside the classroom, the social world of the 'kindergarten class' becomes part of the social worlds each parent is located in during the day. This kind of engagement depends on intensive communication with parents on the part of the teacher. S. makes use of one-to-one conversations and regular email contact in order to inform parents about digital resources and invite them to use various tools. For her, digital networking is especially important because the children usually come to school by bus, which rules out daily personal contact with parents.

S. is aware that not all families have internet access. She has therefore helped families to gain internet access through the local public library. In addition, she offers to print basic information and give it to the children to take home.

Professional changes

For S., the introduction of digital technology in her class is bound up with her own professional development. Using ever more digital technology has been a life-changing experience for her. As she says, the digital tools 'have just completely transformed' her. S. focuses on the connections and possibilities that have arisen from networking. Her professional self has been transformed because she has become (more) publicly visible. Since she has allowed other people to look inside the teaching and learning environments that she has established, her classroom activities are no longer private. She says: 'I always think of my classroom as being open. It's like having a camera on it all day. Whatever we are doing, we really want to share what we are doing'. This statement is not made unconsciously or naïvely, but with a clear awareness of the risks involved. To make oneself publicly visible in this way also means to expose oneself to criticism, whether from parents, other teachers, or administrators. Greater vulnerability is the price that has to be paid for higher visibility, increased feedback, and wider connections. S. describes the principles of a sharing economy in her sphere as follows: to share means to give something and to get something in return. This 'something' does not have to be of material value. Drawing on Belk (2014), this exchange can be seen as an 'open model of education', which replaces the traditional model in which the classroom door remained closed and nobody could see what was happening inside. The proverb: 'You are what you own' thus becomes 'You are what you can share' (Belk 2014). In this sense, S.'s 'value' has risen through the connections she has made by means of digital media. When she was previously locked away in her classroom, nobody was able to see or acknowledge what she was doing. Now that she has become more publicly visible, she has received far more appreciation. Her increased visibility has therefore also changed her professional identity. Here we see a concrete example of the connection between 'representation' and 'identity' in the 'circuit of culture'. This visibility makes it possible for the class to be part of other social worlds or, at least, to increase the intersection between their own world and the others.

In being 'open and transparent', S. herself enters a zone of exchange and her classroom activities become the object of professional exchange. Insofar as she does not see her work as something personal and private, she opens up the possibility of receiving help and support both from people at her own school and from her online communities. S. experiences this support as uncomplicated and enriching as the following quote shows:

> I feel like in our school we have people, resource people that we can go to and talk with them. And I utilized them [...] I have questions or I need help and they help me. Or I put a tweet on Twitter. And say 'Hey, I'm trying this new platform, who should I talk to about this?' And within five minutes I have a ton of responses. [...] And people are so willing to help [...] So I really seek to ask other people to help me with those things that are challenging. Through their assistance and their perspective, my perspective widens.

Both the interviews carried out with parents and our own observations show that S. has also developed several ways of gaining support in the real world. She asks parents to volunteer for group work sessions in the classroom or involves experts in her lessons, delegating certain topics to them. She has been able to gain such support by rejecting the idea that she has to do everything by herself and must not let anyone else see inside the classroom space. This approach is not necessarily connected to the use of digital media. But our case study suggests that the inhibition threshold for seeking external support is probably lowered as a result of the transparency of digital media. Furthermore, digital media can themselves be used to seek out and receive support.

In discussing the use of digital tools – and particularly social networks – in relation to early childhood institutions, one of the elements of the circuit of culture (Hall 1997) is particularly relevant: that of 'regulation'. Despite their apparent authenticity, the social media posts are carefully regulated: certain activities are reported on and others not; the wording is smoothed over; and care is taken to choose an appropriate communication channel. In Goffman's (1999) terms, this selection constitutes a form of 'impression management', since the teacher creates a picture of the children, herself, and the teaching and learning activities they are engaged in. 'Impression management' is not only applicable to digital media, for Goffman developed this concept in the 1950s, before services such as Twitter and Skype could have been envisaged. Nevertheless, digital technology allows impression management to be perfected (Hogan 2010). This insight, however, does not devalue the presentation of kindergarten activities through online media in any way; it only shows that contributions to online platforms are chosen with care and that they are intentionally posted snapshots of everyday life.

The children's perspective

Apparent ease of integration

What is most striking about the children's manipulation of digital media is the apparent ease with which such media can be integrated into the children's activities. Figure 5 shows a typical daily class schedule, of which Twitter forms as integral a part as math or art. The chalkboard also provides information about the types of technology used that day.

The observation showed that the children use digital technology as easily as they use books or worksheets. For them, digital media are a normal part of their kindergarten day, and are not significantly different from other learning materials. During the lessons, the children use the tools and devices provided as a matter of course. For example, when the children were able to choose between different tools – analog and digital – there were no conflicts about who would be allowed to use the tablets first. In addition, the children knew how to handle the tablet without assistance (open the appropriate app, log in and out, use it for writing, taking pictures, or recording an audio sequence). During a lesson in which the class worked with Twitter, the children knew exactly what to do. Using Twitter seemed to have

Figure 5. Timetable on the classroom wall.

the form of a familiar ritual, whose steps were well known. When the class sent out a tweet, a stuffed toy in the shape of the Twitter logo (a bird) was used to symbolize the act. As the children made clear in the interviews, they like this bird a lot.

In one of the interviews, a boy mentioned that he had used Twitter to keep in touch with the class: 'Last Thursday I was sick, that's why I tweeted to them.' We were unable to establish whether it was his idea to tweet with the class or whether it was suggested by his parents; in any case, this example illustrates how digital media may be utilized in order to increase the range of available means of communication. In terms of the theoretical framework of this study, it also shows how the social worlds of 'kindergarten' and 'home' intersect for this boy.

Public visibility as learners

Another example of this normalized use of digital technology is the integration of tablets into math classes, in which the children use several apps to document their learning. The Seesaw app allows them to take a photo of things they have painted or built, and even to add a short (written or spoken) comment or video. The children are able to open the app, log in and out, and save their data by themselves. These skills have of course been developed on the basis of instructions previously provided by the teacher. In addition, when they are unsure of anything the children can look up the relevant details in a book produced by the teacher, which contains screenshots. In the interviews, the children were able to clearly explain the different steps to be taken when using the app by referring to this book.

Nevertheless, the children's lessons still revolve around traditional (analog) activities such as painting, counting, and listening. The use of digital technology is largely adult initiated. The main difference is that the results of these lessons (both products and experiences) are recorded and presented via digital media. It is the children who decide, whether a picture they have painted or a problem they have solved individually is presented via Seesaw or Twitter; thus, the children select what is worth publishing and what is not. In addition, the teacher sometimes suggests posting a Tweet on what the children did. This difference is not just a question of transmission. Through these digital media, the pupils become more publicly visible as learners – both for themselves and their parents. Their work is seen as important and worth recording. The documentation of their working processes and their finished work via digital technology thus provokes reflection on the part of the children – for example, when they show these records to their parents at home.

Parents

Benefits for the children

For the parents, one of the key advantages of digital media is the contribution they make to the children's digital literacy. Manipulating digital tools in several contexts helps the children to become accustomed to this kind of communication. At a concrete level, 'keyboarding skills' were also mentioned, but on the whole parents were rather vague when it came to naming specific skills. The parents describe the manipulation of digital media as a form of meta-skill which ought to strengthen others: 'it's just sharpening their skills'. More broadly, they also see the use of digital media as helping to habituate the children to a digitized world. In the parents' eyes, it is possible for the children to adapt fully to digital technology. They emphasize the possibilities opened up by global communication with children around the world. Here, as well, the parents describe the interlacing of different social worlds as a benefit. This global connectedness was taken to give the children a direct advantage over other children. Its concrete benefits, however, were not clearly delineated. These advantages were expressed in emotional terms (such as 'I really love that'), rather than being clarified rationally.

The comments made by one parent concerning the rationale for using digital media were, however, more concrete. She assumes that digital technology help children to concentrate better.

Another parent widened the perspective when she stated that documenting the children's work in social networks constitutes a form of appreciation: 'I love that the kids do something and for them that posting on their blog is an accomplishment, right, they see their work displayed in another setting and then for us to be able to write comments'.

The pictures of the children's work were also seen as a form of recognition, since parents are able to make comments on them. The parents also referred to another social dimension several times, namely, community belonging. The community here means primarily the class or school community, in which children are members of a peer group. Additionally, it refers to a virtual global community, in which the pupils have 'digital citizenship'. The observation that social networking serves to strengthen community life was also made by Daniel Miller in his study on Facebook (Miller 2013). Miller claims that real interaction is not destroyed but rather facilitated by social networking. The parents here give a similar view, since they regard participation on several digital platforms as an aspect of social affiliation.

We have seen, then, that parents feel there are several advantages for their children in using digital media in the classroom. These include: professional skills (keyboarding skills), methodological skills (connecting with others), personal skills (motivation) und social skills (being part of a community).

Advantages for parents themselves

The parents interviewed also saw digital media as an opportunity to connect with their children. They discuss the possibility of gaining an insight into their child's daily life in the kindergarten. One mother feels that this more intensive contact improves her performance as a mother. This can be understood in terms of a transformation of the notion of parenthood: recent sociological research does not regard the family as a form, but rather as a practice that has to be renewed on a daily basis by those involved (Jurczyk 2014). The task of building a 'community as a system of relations' (ibid., 51) when faced with a lack of time and limited, flexible working hours can be particularly challenging for families. In such a situation, the continual (re-)creation of a shared identity is especially important as a means of strengthening the sense of family belonging (Autenrieth 2014). Previous research has already indicated the possibilities that digital networking offers for multi-local families (Schlör 2012; Theunert and Lange 2012). The parents interviewed in this study also stressed the value of digital networking for traditional families. It offers parents who work full-time the opportunity to become more involved in family life through the insights it provides into the everyday lives of the children. Fathers in particular, who are often excluded from kindergarten or school life through their professional activities, are offered new ways to take part in their children's upbringing, as one mother explains:

> I'm the one who is in the classroom and always go on field trips…it's easier for him. It's easier during the day. It comes to both of us and he often comes home and says: 'Oh, did you see the post on Kidblog,' or: 'Did you see the things that S. [the teacher] tweeted'. And I often say: 'No, I didn't had chance to sit down and look at it' [...] I think it helps them [the fathers] to get more involved, for sure. Or even, you know, in my family it definitely helps my husband to be involved, but I think if you have two working parents, it's a wonderful thing.

Thus far, research has primarily focused on families' own posts, interpreting these as an externalization of private events or experiences (Ammari et al. 2015). The present study, by contrast, shows how posts addressed to families by pupils and teachers contribute to family cohesion by providing transparency and visibility. The insights provided into the child's world can serve as a stimulus for conversation between parents and children. The aim of the digital representation of educational activities is closely linked to that of pedagogical documentation, which seeks to involve parents in their children's learning and to stimulate a form of partnership-based cooperation between families and educational institutions (Knauf 2015).

Parents' own digital media skills

It is not only the children's skills that are enhanced through greater use of digital media, but also the parents'. In order to take part in the children's digital activities, the parents need internet access and appropriate devices. By choosing certain online platforms, the teacher pushes parents to learn how to use them. Nevertheless, the capacity of these online tools to involve parents is limited. Not all of the parents have internet access, or even the required language skills. During the interviews, the children were explicitly asked about the use of online platforms at home. Some of the children stated that they used these platforms with their parents. Only one child said that his parents 'don't have Twitter at home', so they were not able to look at the things he posted: 'my parents really don't know how to talk like this, they talk Chinese'. Here, certain exclusion mechanisms based on access and language barriers become evident. In fact, these mechanisms are not restricted to digital media, but would play a part in any form of verbal communication. What becomes clear here, however, is that digital technology does not serve to automatically eliminate these exclusionary factors.

Alongside technical barriers, there are also other barriers that can prevent parents from becoming more closely involved with their children's education. The parents interviewed in this study felt that digital media both offered them new opportunities and made significant demands on them. They felt there was an expectation that parents would look at digital media posts and comment on and react to them. Parents also found that the number of communication channels available could be overwhelming and that the expectations placed on them put them under pressure. Both interviewees describe this feeling as typical at the beginning of the kindergarten year. Nevertheless, the parents also state that this attitude toward the huge variety of digital media on offer gradually changes. The pressure and the feeling of 'urgency' dissolve. The parents develop strategies to help prevent information overload. One parent put her own strategy in the form of a piece of advice:

> Do what you can. Find the things that are easier for you to do. If you can't handle tweeting at home, that's ok. Follow the blog. Just take what you can handle and do. It's just an offer. Take the things that she offers and take the things that you feel very comfortable doing and take enjoyment in those things and that's ok. Maybe later in the year you'll find more time or you become more comfortable, maybe not.

This parent clearly notes that the opportunity to use the different platforms has to be seen as an offer. The parents interviewed during the study recognize this and act accordingly.

A further potential problem is the protection of personal data and privacy. This point was not raised by the parents on their own initiative, but in response to the interviewer's questions. In Germany, for example, the use of digital media and social networks in educational contexts is almost exclusively discussed with regard to privacy protection (for a detailed discussion of this see: Miller 2013). Parents in Germany may well have reservations about digital media usage, particularly where public platforms are concerned. This emphasis on privacy protection seems rather odd to the parents interviewed for the present study. Since they are on Facebook themselves, they feel quite familiar with digital technology and social networks. In addition, they place a great deal of trust in the teacher's discretion. S., they feel, takes great care where security is concerned – for example by not posting names, as the following quote shows:

> I'm ok with that. She ensures that there are no names used. I'm ok with that because there's no personal information. [...] There are photos of children everywhere. You open up our local newspaper, there's photos... so, I feel like, as long as there is enough caution to be taken it can't be traced back to where his classroom is and where we live, I'm ok with that. I do trust especially with S., she is so vigilant with how she uses these tools.

The parents' consent to the publication of pictures is thus clearly not based on indifference or *naïveté*. It is rooted rather in their confidence in the teacher and their own experience with digital media.

To summarize: the parents are highly appreciative of the teacher's use of digital media in their children's kindergarten. They see these different ways of getting involved in the children's kindergarten experience as an opportunity to support the children's learning and strengthen their community. Digital media allow working parents in particular to play a greater role in their children's upbringing. On the other hand, however, these media can also have an exclusionary character, since they require certain linguistic and technological skills, as well as Internet access and time.

Conclusion

The present paper told the story of a kindergarten class in which a number of digital media were applied on a daily basis to enhance children's learning. This was also a story of mediatization, in which digital media were seen to have a transformative effect on communication.

These media have changed both the quality and quantity of communication in the kindergarten. First, the volume of communication has increased. Pupils post on digital platforms on a daily basis, and the teacher communicates with parents several times a week. Prior to the introduction of digital technology in the classroom, the teacher communicated with parents roughly once a week by mail, whereas now there is a high level of reciprocal communication. Second, the quality of the communication has changed. The connection is no longer a one-way street, since parents respond to the children's posts or initiate conversations themselves.

Furthermore, the children are often no longer simply the subject of this conversation; through their posts on the various online platforms they have also become active participants in it. This links up to an important step described in the research literature: online contexts give children the opportunity not only to consume, but also to produce content (Waller 2013). This is why the relationship between children and adults has begun to change as well; when children are able to make their voices heard (whether through videos, audio messages, or images) they can exert a more direct influence on relationships.

The fact that learning processes and their results are seen as worthy of being recorded via digital technology, and thereby made available to a wider audience, serves to increase their value. This has consequences for all those involved in the kindergarten examined here: The teacher's status is enhanced since her pedagogical innovations can be shared with other teachers, and parents can also gain an insight into her activities. The value of the children's work also increases, since they come to be seen as active learners and serious conversation partners where their own learning is concerned. Finally, the parents are no longer simply addressed by the teacher but become collaborators in the children's development. In this way, the identities of all those involved in this kindergarten class have been changed through the utilization of digital media, which is typical for mediatization processes. According to the participants' descriptions, this social world now seems to be characterized by greater visibility, transparency, and togetherness. Thus, the social world of this kindergarten class has changed in itself, but it has also changed the way it interacts with the outside world by connecting with other social worlds. These achievements do not come for free. A willingness to learn, a preparedness to be publicly visible, and a significant investment of time – especially on the part of the adults – are all essential.

Disclosure statement

No potential conflict of interest was reported by the author.

ORCID

Helen Knauf http://orcid.org/0000-0002-7690-6218

References

Ammari, Tawfiq, Priya Kumar, Cliff Lampe, Sarita Schoenebeck. 2015. "Managing Children's Online Identities: How Parents Decide What to Disclose About Their Children Online." In *Proceedings of the 33rd Annual SIGCHI Conference on Human Factors in Computing Systems (CHI '15)*, edited by Bo Begole, Jinwoo Kim, Kori Inkpen and Woontack Wo, 1895–1904. New York: ACM Press. doi:10.1145/2702123.2702325.

Aufenanger, Stefan. 2015. "Wie die Neuen Medien Kindheit verändern." [How New Media Change Childhood.] In *Wischen Klicken Knipsen* [Swipe, Click, Snap], edited by Günther Anfang, Kathrin Demmler, Klaus Lutz, and Kati Struckmeyer, 205–210. München: Kopaed.

Autenrieth, Ulla. 2014. "Die, Digital Natives' Präsentieren Ihre Kinder." [The 'digital natives' present their children.] *Studies in Communication Sciences* 14: 99–107. doi:10.1016/j.scoms.2014.12.006.

Belk, Russell. 2014. "You are what you can access: Sharing and collaborative consumption online." *Journal of Business Research* 67 (8): 1595–1600. doi:10.1016/j.jbusres.2013.10.001.

Beschorner, Beth, and Amy Hutchinson. 2013. "iPads as a Literacy Teaching Tool in Early Childhood." *International Journal of Education in Mathematics, Science and Technology* 1 (1): 16–24.

Blackwell, Courtney K., Alexis R. Lauricella, and Ellen Wartella. 2014. "Factors Influencing Digital Technology Use in Early Childhood Education." *Computers & Education* 77 (August): 82–90. doi:10.1016/j.compedu.2014.04.013.

Buckingham, David. 2013. *Beyond Technology: Children's Learning in the Age of Digital Culture*. Cambridge: Wiley.

Burnett, Cathy, and Karen Daniels. 2016. "Technology and Literacy in the Early Years. Framing Young Children's Meaning-making with New Technologies." In *Understanding Digital Technologies and Young Children*, edited by Susanne Garvis and Narelle Lemon, 18–27. London: Routledge.

Clark, Cindy D. 2010. *In A Younger Voice*. Oxford: Oxford University Press.

Danby, S., C. Davidson, L. M. Given, and K. Thorpe. 2016. "Composing an Email. Social Interaction in a Preschool Classroom." In *Understanding Digital Technologies and Young Children*, edited by Susanne Garvis and Narelle Lemon, 5–17. London: Routledge.

Endepohls-Ulpe, Martina, Claudia Quaiser-Pohl, and Christine Deckers. 2016. "Availability and Use of Personal Computers in German Kindergarten." In *Understanding Digital Technologies and Young Children*, edited by Susanne Garvis and Narelle Lemon, 112–121. Predictions and Influences. London: Routledge.

European Commission. 2015. *Young Children (0–8) and Digital Technology*. Luxemburg: Publications Office of the European Union.

Flick, Uwe. 2014. *An Introduction to Qualitative Research*. London: Sage.

Goffman, Erving. 1999. *The Presentation of Self in Everyday Life*. Gloucester: Peter Smith Pub Incorporated.

Hall, Stuart. 1997. "Introduction." In *Representation: Cultural Representations and Signifying Practices*, edited by Stuart Hall, 1–12. London: SAGE Publications.

Hogan, B. 2010. "The Presentation of Self in the Age of Social Media: Distinguishing Performances and Exhibitions Online." *Bulletin of Science, Technology & Society* 30 (6): 377–386. SAGE Publications. doi:10.1177/0270467610385893.

Jurczyk, Karin. 2014. "Familie als Herstellungsleistung." [Family as a manufactured product.] In *Doing Family - Familienalltag heute: Warum Familienleben nicht mehr selbstverständlich ist* [Doing Family – Family Life Today: Why Family Life Can't be Taken for Granted], edited by Karin Jurczyk, Andreas Lange and Barbara Thiessen, 50–70. Weinheim: Juventa.

Keane, Therese, William F. Keane, and Aaron S. Blicblau. 2014. "Beyond Traditional Literacy: Learning and Transformative Practices Using ICT." *Education and Information Technologies*September. Springer, 19: 1–13. doi:10.1007/s10639-014-9353-5.

Knauf, Helen. 2015. "Styles of Documentation in German Early Childhood Education." *Early Years* 35: 1–17. March. Routledge. doi:10.1080/09575146.2015.1011066.

Krotz, Friedrich. 2015. "Mediatisierung" [Mediatization]. In *Handbuch Cultural Studies und Medienanalyse* [Handbook Cultural Studies and Media Analysis], edited by Andreas Hepp, Friedrich Krotz, Swantje Lingenberg, and Jeffrrey Wimmer, 439–451. Wiesbaden: Springer. doi:10.1007/978-3-531-19021-1_45.

Marsh, Jackie, Peter Hannon, Margaret Lewis, and Louise Ritchie. 2015. "Young Children's Initiation Into Family Literacy Practices in the Digital Age." *Journal of Early Childhood Research*, June. SAGE Publications, 13, 1476718X15582095. doi:10.1177/1476718X15582095.

Mascheroni, Giovanna, and Kjartan Ólafsson. 2015. "The Mobile Internet: Access, Use, Opportunities and Divides Among European Children." *New Media & Society*, January. SAGE, 17: 1–23. doi:10.1177/1461444814567986.

McManis, Lilla D., and Susan B. Gunnewig. 2012. "Finding the Education in Educational Technology with Early Learners." *Young Children* 5: 14–24. doi:10.1016/j.compedu.2014.04.013.

Miller, Daniel. 2013. *Tales From Facebook*. Cambridge: Wiley.

Palaiologou, Ioanna. 2016. "Children Under Five and Digital Technologies: Implications for Early Years Pedagogy." *European Early Childhood Education Research Journal*, February, 24: 5–24. doi:10.1080/1350293X.2014.929876.

Plowman, Lydia, Joanna McPake, and Christine Stephen. 2010. "The Technologisation of Childhood? Young Children and Technology in the Home." *Children & Society* 24 (1): 63–74.

Röser, Jutta, Corinna Peil. 2012. "Das Zuhause als mediatisierte Welt im Wandel. Fallstudien und Befunde zur Domestizierung des Internets als Mediatisierungsprozess". [Home as Mediatized World. Case Studies and Findings on Domestication of the Internet as a Process of Mediatization.] In *Mediatisierte Welten* [Mediatized Worlds], edited by Friedrich Krotz and Andreas Hepp, 137–163. Wiesbaden: VS Verlag. doi:10.1007/978-3-531-94332-9_6

Roulston, Kathryn. 2010. *Reflective Interviewing*. Los Angeles, CA: SAGE Publications.

Schlör, Karin. 2012. "Wo is n dein Papa? – Im Skype, ne? Doing Family und intergenerative Medienbildung im Kontext von Multilokalität." [Where's your Dad? Inside Skype, Right? Doing Family and Intergenerational Media Literacy in the Context of Multilocality.] *Merz Wissenschaft* 57–66.

Scifo, Barbara. 2015. "Investigating the Domestication of Convergent Mobile Media and Mobile Internet by Children and Teens." *New Media & Society* 17 (10): 1603–1623. doi:10.1177/1461444814530291.

Strauss, Anselm. 1978. "A Social World Perspective." *Studies in Symbolic Interaction* 1: 119–128.

Theunert, Helga, and Andreas Lange. 2012. "'Doing Family' im Zeitalter von Mediatisierung und Pluralisierung." [Doing Family in the Age of Mediatization and Pluralization.] *Merz. Zeitschrift Für Medienpädagogik* 56 (2): 10–21.

Waller, Martin. 2013. "More than Tweets. Developing the 'New' and the 'Old' through Online Networking." In *Virtual Literacies: Interactive Spaces for Children and Young People*, edited by Guy Merchant, Julia Gillen, Jackie Marsh and Julia Davies, 126–141. New York: Routledge.

Wartella, Ellen, Roberta L Schomburg, Alexis R Lauricella, Michael Robb, Rachel Flynn. 2010. *Technology in the Lives of Teachers and Classrooms*. http://cmhd.northwestern.edu/wp-content/uploads/2015/10/TechInTheLivesofTeachers-1.pdf.

Yelland, Nicola. 2016. "iPlay, iLearn, iGrow." In *Understanding Digital Technologies and Young Children*, edited by Susanne Garvis and Narelle Lemon, 122–138. London: Routledge. Tablet Technologies, Curriculum, Pedagogies and Learning in the Twenty-First Century.

Yin, Robert K. 2009. *Case Study Research*. London: Sage.

An ecological exploration of young children's digital play: framing children's social experiences with technologies in early childhood

Lorna Arnott

ABSTRACT
This article outlines an ecological framework for describing children's social experiences during digital play. It presents evidence from a study that explored how 3- to 5-year-old children negotiated their social experiences as they used technologies in preschool. Utilising a systematic and iterative cycle of data collection and analysis, children's interactions with 24 technological resources were examined over a nine-month period and across three phases. Findings reveal that children played in clusters, exhibiting a multitude of social behaviours and interactions and varied degrees of social participation, and assumed various social status roles and technological positions. These behaviours formed part of a Digital Play System, which in turn was influenced by the Preschool System, which comprises children and practitioners as active agents, technological affordances, and the cultural systems, routines and practices of the early childhood setting. Ultimately, children's social experiences during digital play cannot be determined by any single element of the ecological system.

Introduction

Contemporary explorations of technology use in early years' education have progressed significantly in the last decade. We are seeing exciting movements away from narrowly defined explorations of children's interactions with specific resources, towards broader investigations of the role and position of technologies within children's early learning experiences. Research is beginning to describe how technologies form one part of the complex ecological system of children's early learning. This account describes how play experiences are being re-imagined in early childhood (Yelland 2010) and how digital play may be explored or investigated in new ways (Edwards 2013). For example, the use of technologies in all aspects of early childhood is being explored, widening the earlier focus on technology use in formal educational settings (Plowman 2015; Plowman et al. 2012). These ecological explorations are facilitated by broader definitions of technologies which move beyond screen-based media (Arnott 2013) to consider working and non-working technologies (Bird, forthcoming). Similarly, increasing theorisation – such as the presentation of a Digital Play Framework (Bird and Edwards 2014) – is helping researchers and practitioners to understand the role of technologies in children's lives, culture and play.

This paper contributes to this evolving body of literature by presenting a techno-ecological framework to explore children's social experiences during digital play. Ecological research about children's social experiences, interactions and behaviours in preschool was widely available in the 1980s but this focus is underdeveloped in contemporary technological studies. Lingering and often unsubstantiated moral panics continue to influence the portrayal of technologies as deterministically shaping interactions (e.g. Rowan 2015). In order to challenge these assertions, more evidence is needed of the multitude of contextual and social factors that contribute to young children's experiences of using technologies. This is particularly the case as research demonstrates that technologies are embedded in cultural contexts, resulting in calls for explorations of the wider ecologies of children's digital play (Livingstone et al. 2015). This paper contributes to this perspective by presenting a framework of some of the key contextual and social factors that shaped children's social experiences in a study of 3–5 year olds' digital play.

Technologies as tools in digital play and pedagogies

As technologies have become ubiquitous in life, work and leisure, questions are continually raised about how these resources may be transforming childhood experiences. Concerns were once raised about the developmental appropriateness of such resources (Cordes and Miller 2000). This was particularly evident with the integration of screen-based media into childhood and early education. The concerns were related to the long history in ecological and human geography literature of exploring the link between toys and children's social interactions and experiences. These perspectives suggest a link between environment and social experiences, behaviours and play (Read, Sugawara, and Brandt 1999). Such perspectives have extended into Education literature and we see popular theorising from approaches like Reggio Emilia that recognise links between the physical environment and children's development and play (Strong-Wilson and Ellis 2007). Specific toys and artefacts form part of this broad discussion, for example a link between resources being 'social' and 'isolate' – i.e. designed for individual or social use – is discussed (Driscoll and Carter 2009). The general understanding is that certain resources and artefacts encourage social interaction while others inhibit it (Chandler, Fowler, and Lubeck 1992). For example, dolls, games and dramatic play materials have been linked to more cooperative play or social interaction, while art activities and puzzles have been linked to more solitary or parallel play (Rubin 1977). For technological resources, questions around their affordances for children's play have consistently been raised, though only relatively recently in relation to empirical evidence.

In recent years, theorising around digital technologies in early childhood has begun to re-evaluate the deterministic link between objects and behaviours or learning outcomes. For example, contemporary research on creativity in a digital age points to the *possibilities* afforded by technologies, rather than deterministic outcomes (Craft 2012). The focus is on the child as empowered to manipulate and interpret technological tools in multiple ways. Similarly, Brooker and Siraj-Blatchford (2002, 19) showed that young children do not distinguish between screen-based media and concrete toys in the way that adults do, rather they treat them in a similar manner and as such 'manipulation of symbols and images on the computer screen represents a new form of symbolic play'. These perspectives began to position children as active, rather than passive, in the technological experience; a fundamental shift in thinking, informed by sociological perspectives on childhood which consider children to be active agents, shaping their own destinies (James and James 2004).

We are now beginning to see evidence of pedagogical advances in early childhood practices which locate the child at the centre of the learning experience, embodying agency to drive and determine their own outcomes, even with technologies. These ideas are seen in play-based pedagogies and child-initiated learning (whether around traditional or digital resources) which focus on children learning and developing through experience, collaboration and interaction, with the environment but also with peers (Fisher 2008; Woods 2013). They are embedded in sociocultural approaches which see the social and individual as an inseparable dualism where knowledge is co-constructed through social interactions (Rogoff et al. 1993; Vygotsky 1978). This brings to the fore the need to understand the wider context within which children are playing with technologies as well as children's social play experiences around these resources.

The broader focus on children's social play in early childhood is not new. Frameworks for observing and classifying social play experiences are readily available, including Parten's (1932) Social Participation Framework and Broadhead's (2010) Social Play Continuum. Both seek to describe children's increasing progression of sociability in their play through the actions and behaviours they exhibit. Yet few studies have made links between these models and children's technological play. Similarly, given the complexity associated with children's social play, studies often explore these experiences in their own right, or in relation to one element of the ecological environment (e.g. the focus on toys as presented above). Yet evidence shows that children's social play cannot be devoid of context and in many cases is part of a complex matrix of factors which shape children's experience (Arnott 2013). A fuller framework is needed to bring together the different elements of the social context which contribute to children's digital play.

Another recent direction for research has been discussion of the Digital Consumerist Context (Edwards 2013), which emphasises children's right to participate in the evolving digital economy. This approach describes how children's contemporary play experiences are located within a cultural historical context which affords new ways of consuming, and playing with, media. Product designers, engineers, practitioners and researchers are acutely aware of the early childhood technological 'market' and technologies are being designed with younger users in mind. Developments in touch screen technologies, for example, have eliminated many of the early motor and dexterity challenges that children faced when using more traditional technologies. Increased policy drivers around STEM (science, technology, engineering and maths) in education and society have promoted the development of resources which seek to foster early engineers or computer programmers, such as early programming blocks (Bers and Horn 2010). Similarly, as we move into the era of gamification of education (Nolan and McBride 2014) and a period where creativity is valued in education and society, we are seeing an increased interest in open-world games as part of children's learning experiences in school.

All of these developments feed in to the increased focus on play-based pedagogies for developing children's use of technologies. Attention has shifted towards establishing how we can best support children in early learning and development by integrating technologies in playful ways (Bird and Edwards 2014; Edwards 2013; Marsh 2010). Parents want to know how best to support their children in their technological endeavours and practitioners and teachers want guidance on how to integrate technologies into their pedagogies (Palaiologou 2014). In early years, this has generated an interest in children's digital play.

In light of these new ways of positioning children's technological experiences, an understanding of digital play-based pedagogies is vital. In place of a deterministic perspective which views technologies as driving forces in children's lives, we need to seek to position children's technologies within contemporary sociocultural and contextual frames. By focusing on a techno-ecological model of children's digital play, this paper offers a starting point for this process. The framework presented below offers some insights into the factors that practitioners may consider when planning for children's digital play experiences. It does not claim to offer a pedagogical model that practitioners can adopt; rather it gives an overview of key contextual and social factors that shape children's social experiences during digital play and thus offers a route for practitioners to critically reflect on these elements of the preschool context in order to inform their own digital pedagogies.

Methodology and methods

The purpose of the study was to explore children's social experiences during their digital play in early childhood settings. This study was informed by a Contextualist perspective in the sense that it considers 'phenomena as being inherently situated within context' (Packer and Scott, 1992, 108). It is therefore concerned with exploring various aspects of context as well as the relationships and connections between these aspects. Importantly, from a Contextualist perspective, the nature of reality cannot solely be understood through a realist ontology which assumes that structures influence each other in a cause-and-effect manner. Under Contextualist thinking, reality is not 'out there' waiting to be uncovered; rather it involves a level of interpretation and construction on the part of the individual. It therefore adopts elements of relativist ontology and within this frame, multiple realities are considered to exist depending upon the 'social, economic, cultural and historic nature of the group under consideration' (Tudge et al. 2009, 118). Similarly, activities vary depending upon features of the individuals, the setting and the cultural and temporal context (Tudge et al. 2006; Tudge et al. 2009). In light of this perspective, the study was guided by the question: *What ecological factors in early childhood playrooms contributed to children's social experiences during their digital play?*

Data were collected from two preschools in central Scotland. The preschools were chosen because of their different approaches to technology integration, with one nursery representing 'typical' technological provision in the area and the other involving staff who had received specific training in framing technological experiences for children. The nurseries also differed in size and available space. One offered a large open planned space, while the other offered a more cosy and confined environment for children's play, particularly as the space was divided into two smaller rooms (although free flow between the rooms was encouraged). Both settings focused on 3–5 provision and the research took place in the main playroom. Scottish Educational Research Association ethical guidelines (SERA 2005) were followed and iterative institutional ethical approval was granted for this project.

Approximately 90 children were involved in the project, across the two settings. Data were collected across a nine-month period and the same cohorts of children were observed on multiple occasions during these visits (although different children often chose to use the resources during each visit). I visited morning or afternoon sessions spanning 3 h. Overall,

Table 1. Technologies observed.

Technology
Computer
Interactive Whiteboard
Leappad
Laptop
Alphabet Board
Electronic Bus
Electronic Road
Fire Truck
Landline Telephone
Microwave
Mobile Telephone
Shopping Till
Hair Straighteners
Washing Machine
Digital Cameras
Metal Detector
Fairy Lights
Calculator
Exercise Equipment
CD Player
Musical Keyboard
Tape Recorder
Duplo Techs
Tool Box

a child-led approach was adopted where children's participation in various activities was wholly dependent on individual children's desire to take part at any given time. Children drifting in and out of researcher-led games displayed a fluid process which was typical of their early play experiences in preschool (Moyles 2014).

Parents were not present during the observed preschool sessions but practitioners were sometimes involved in the children's play. In the majority of cases, the observation focused on child–child experiences as practitioner involvement in the play was infrequent. The researcher provided no guidance about how children should play with technologies, instead spontaneous interactions were encouraged in order to observe children's technological experiences in a naturalistic manner.

A broad definition of technologies provided the context to observe children's experiences. Children were not provided with any technological resources to use as part of the project; instead, observations were conducted around any technologies that were readily available within each setting. This meant that observations varied across the settings depending upon the technologies that were available. Table 1 demonstrates some of the technologies observed in use in the two preschools. A focal-technology approach was adopted so that observations were centred around the specific resources available for a designated time and not around case study children. This allowed for an understanding of how children's interactions and experiences continually fluctuated as children and practitioners entered and left the play space around the technology.

Data were collected via systematic observations, cluster mapping (noting down each child's location, activity and social interaction on a classroom map), researcher-led games and interviews with practitioners. Details of each of the methods employed and the volume of data collected can be found elsewhere (Arnott 2013). The observations and cluster mapping offered an insight into children's digital play processes. The researcher-led games had two purposes: (1) to understand children's perspectives about the structure of the setting; (2) to decipher how their experiences with technologies were shaped by the physical and social structure in place. The interviews with staff provided an alternative viewpoint on the structural systems in place within the environment, which may have contributed to children's play with technologies.

The children's digital play was observed on any occasion when children voluntarily decided to use the resources. In both settings, children were advised that I was writing a story about their play with technologies so they were familiar with my purpose, and they were asked for verbal consent for their activities to be observed and included in my 'story'. The number of observations for each child varied, dependent upon their voluntary involvement throughout the visits. This in itself provided a useful insight into their preferences for resources as well as giving some methodological insights into how to engage children in the research process.

In terms of the more structured activities (researcher-led games) children volunteered to take part. These approaches were described as games to reflect the playful nature of the data collection techniques, which were designed in a child-centred manner to mirror many of the activities that children would typically complete in preschools. They were framed to children as games and activities, not 'play' in the traditional sense which is considered spontaneous and child-led. The children were aware that completing the games meant that they would contribute to the story about their experiences with technologies. Children could complete the games and not have their data included in the research but no children expressed this desire. The researcher was set up at a table in the middle of the playroom and children approached to ask the researcher about the game. After a brief explanation, children either opted in or out and the researcher confirmed the child's willingness to participate and to be included in the 'story'. Since participation was entirely voluntary, not all children completed the games, and so those involved in the researcher-led games were not necessarily the same as the children who were observed during digital free play.

Due to the exploratory nature of the study, iterative analysis after each session informed the next session and, where appropriate, changes were made to the data collection approach. Initial visits focused on systematic observations and cluster mapping procedures. Mid-way through data collection the researcher-led games were introduced. Interviews with staff were conducted in the concluding phases.

This project aimed to consider what factors shaped children's social experiences with technologies. Qualitative inquiry (Creswell 2012) provided this rich data. Previous analysis of this data-set focused on children's social behaviours and Broadhead's (2010) Social Play Continuum was used to code children's interactions and behaviour. This paper, however, draws on previous knowledge of pedagogies for supporting use of technologies in the early years (Plowman and Stephen 2007) and was concerned with both distal and proximal influences on children's digital play. In addition, as the data collection progressed, the role of structure and agency within the setting became paramount. Data were stored in terms of episodes and categorised according to the three areas:

(1) the role of the children as agents;
(2) technological affordances; and
(3) the social and cultural framing of children's activities within preschool systems.

While the themes and codes were undoubtedly influenced by my previous theoretical knowledge, the analysis for this paper was in essence grounded in the data.

Theoretical guide to analysis

Analysis of the data for this project, from an ecological perspective, was influenced by Bronfenbrenner's ecological systems theory (Bronfenbrenner 1994), particularly the latter developments around proximal processes (Bronfenbrenner 1995). It was important to recognise the preschool setting as a system, with many interlinking and multifaceted components that were woven together; in this case *person* (children and practitioners), *process* (children's digital play interactions) and *context* (both physical, social and cultural). It should be noted that *time*, Bronfenbrenner's fourth component, is not considered here as individual children were not tracked over a longitudinal period and the study did not form case studies of individual children's technology use across the project.

Ecology in this paper is used in a broad sense. The discussion is not limited to the physical space but seeks to address the interplay between the physical, social and cultural elements of the environment (physical, social and cultural). The paper moves away from the notion that technological affordances shape behaviour directly, and includes also the children's own motives and attitudes (Walmsley and Lewis 2014), which contribute to their social interactions and experiences during digital play. Ecology here describes the overlapping and interacting elements of the preschool contexts, including agency, structure and the physical as well as social spaces that shape children's experiences with technologies.

Results and discussion

The key findings from this project suggest that children's social experiences during digital play are shaped by two interconnected systems which can be labelled the 'Digital Play System' and the 'Preschool System'. I begin by presenting these as two distinct systems for ease of explanation but as will become clear, these systems actually overlap and are interconnected. It is this complete system (see Figure 3) that is offered as a techno-ecological framework for exploring children's social experiences during digital play.

The Digital Play System

The Digital Play System (presented in Figure 1) describes the directly observable behaviours, interactions and negotiation processes that children engaged in when using technologies. It represents the immediate and immersive context of children's digital play and begins to unpick the characteristics of children's digital play from a social perspective. From an ecological systems theory perspective, it could be viewed as one representation of the proximal processes involved in children's digital play; a microcosm of activity which occurs within the preschool microsystem. It can be thought of as a nano-system which describes children's observable digital play.

Figure 1 illustrates the complex nature of children's social experiences during digital play, as observed in this study. It is essential to start by stating that children's digital play predominantly took place in clusters. Clusters are described as 'multiple children standing in close proximity to the resource and attempting to take part in some way, even if not physically

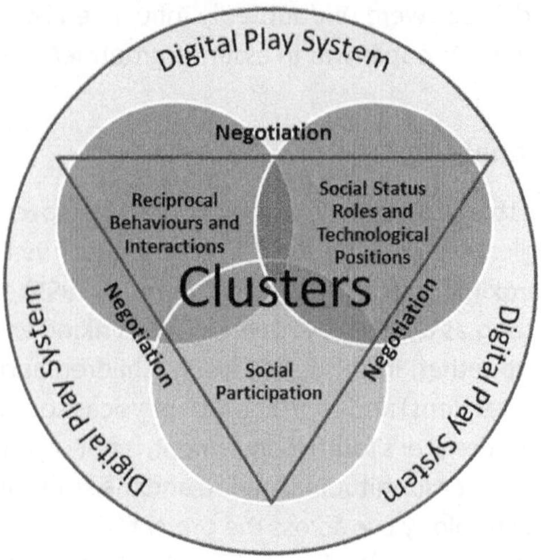

Figure 1. The Digital Play System.

controlling the technology' (Arnott 2013, 101). Five characteristics could be used to describe the clusters:

(1) Close physical proximity to a technological resource (see Table 1), although technologies could be integrated into play themes alongside non-digital resources as well;
(2) Members were focused/engaged with other children in the group, the technology or both;
(3) Membership was dynamic and changing with children entering and leaving;
(4) Membership involved 2 or more children (typically 2–10 children);
(5) Sub-clusters could develop.

These clusters were the heart of all digital play and they provided the foundation for interaction and social engagement to occur. When isolated or solitary play did occur, it lasted for a matter of minutes. The free choice nature of children's preschool day and child-centred pedagogies meant that children were quickly joined by new playmates. The clusters were therefore in a constant state of flux as children entered and left.

This continual evolution of clusters is vital to the direction of development of children's digital play experiences. When working from a Contextualist perspective, it must be recognised that the interplay between the person and context is fundamental to the progression of the play. Thus, as children bring with them very different experiences, knowledge, motivations and attitudes towards technologies, the play is continually transformed and redirected, as a result of the particular composition of the cluster at any given time. An ongoing process of negotiation between peers, and between children and technology, facilitated this continual transformation of clusters and helped to describe children's social experiences during digital play in relation to three elements:

(1) The reciprocal behaviours and interactions that children exhibited;
(2) Children's Social Participation; and
(3) The Matrix of Social Status Roles and Technological Positions which children adopted.

Reciprocal behaviours and interactions

Analysis of the data revealed that the children demonstrated three categories of engagement (pro-social, anti-social and task-driven), during which nine forms of social interactions and 27 behaviours/actions were observed. Broadhead's Social Play Continuum (Broadhead 2010) was used to begin this analysis and when combined with the grounded data, Table 1 was developed which illustrates the observed engagement, behaviours and interactions exhibited. Multiple behaviours and interactions were exhibited within each observed episode as the clusters evolved and changed.

The interactions and behaviours were apparently unpredictable and no discernible patterns could be established. Nevertheless, it was possible to say that typically, children attempted to establish interactions and their experiences were predominantly pro-social. Children actively sought out interactions and they frequently exhibited helping behaviours and scaffolded their peers' learning with technology. Children rarely exhibited anti-social interactions and when negative interactions were observed they usually revolved around children's desire to establish or maintain access to the technological resources.

The variability of children's behaviours and interactions was one of the first findings that prompted the focus on the wider ecological context around children's digital play. It quickly became apparent that neither technologies nor the children in isolation determined children's social experiences during digital play.

Children's Social Participation

Despite not being able to determine a clear pattern of interactions and behaviours, it was at least possible to discern that patterns for Social Participation (Parten 1932) could be either: fleeting, sustained or contingent on context. More specifically, it became clear that children's Solitary Play was often 'fleeting' in that it occurred often, in around 51% of focus-technology observations, but lasted for mere minutes before those children were joined by new play partners. Parallel and Associative Play was more sustained. Such play occurred less often but when it was evident it could continue for long periods. Cooperative Play however was highly contingent upon context and framing of the play experience, and was influenced by the varied elements of both the Digital Play System and the Preschool System. It was clear that multiple forms of participation could be observed within one digital play episode as clusters evolved and changed.

The finding that cooperative play was highly contingent on the play context once again led to the need for an exploration of the influence of the wider ecological context in shaping children's social experiences during digital play.

The Matrix of Social Status Roles and technological positions

The Matrix of Social Status Roles is discussed at length elsewhere (please see Arnott 2013). Nevertheless, it is important here to point out that within clusters, children's ability to recognise and act upon their roles and positions in relation to the rest of the group, and in relation to the technology was one more factor which shaped how the social experiences emerged in their digital play.

Fundamentally, it was evident that children themselves had considerable agency in shaping their own digital play. Yet this agency was often constrained or moulded by the child's position in relation to the technology as well as their role within the clusters. The work of Ljung-Djärf (2008) was used, and adapted, in data analysis to describe the range of technological positions assumed by children in clusters, including owner, spectator, parallel owners and mutual owners. These technological positions contributed to how they *interacted with the technology*. For example, whether the children physically controlled the resources, observed other children using the resource, or for technologies which had multiple parts and functions whether multiple children could collaboratively control the resource:

> Technologies that afforded collaborative use (e.g. the interactive whiteboard) often resulted in mutual ownership. The interactive whiteboard allowed two or more children to control the large screen simultaneously. Similarly, a nearby desktop computer powered the interactive whiteboard and enabled one child to control the computer while another operated the touch screen whiteboard at the same time. These observations suggest that, using multi-functional technologies can reduce conflict by enabling a number of children to work at the same time. (Arnott 2013, 104–105)

Similarly, as indicated in literature on peer leadership (Parten 1933; Shin et al. 2004) it was possible to see that in addition to technological positions, children also assumed social status roles including leader, interacting member and non-interacting member. These roles contributed to how children *interacted with peers around technology*. For example, whether they controlled and directed the other children, spoke to or gestured to other children in a more collegiate manner or whether they were physically present with no interpersonal interaction, as demonstrated in the extract of data below.

> Three boys have formed a cluster around the computer. Chris is controlling the computer by using the mouse. Harvey is sitting next to him in front of the computer and Steven is hovering close by. Harvey offers encouragement to Chris, 'You got 10!' he shouts with an excited tone. Steven becomes more and more excited with this activity and begins to show it by bouncing up and down while he stands next to the computer. He begins to cheer. Suddenly, Harvey turns to Steven and sharply says 'Shhh- Don't do that!'. Steven is immediately silent and observes quietly. (E24h, Harvey aged 4, Computer) (Arnott 2013, 105–106)

Fundamentally, the data indicated that children assumed both technological positions and social status roles simultaneously and when combined, they influenced the degree of agency for the child in relation to the rest of the cluster or to the technology, or both, depending upon the combination adopted.

The Digital Play System: how children negotiate their social experiences around technologies

The Digital Play System – as part of a wider techno-ecological framework –describes the kinds of social experiences that children engage with and exhibit in preschools during their digital play. It offers an insight into how children operate as part of a cluster, constantly negotiating with other children and the technologies during their play to arrive at a multitude of social behaviours and interactions; degrees of social participation; and social status roles and technological positions.

These theoretical concepts are not new, yet the assembly of this data together in relation to technological experiences, and particularly from a social perspective, is novel. It is the process of cluster development and continual negotiation between children, and between child and technology, that is significant when considering this system.

The Digital Play System presents only one element in the puzzle. It demonstrates the processes that children engage in during their digital play but in many cases, it still fails to articulate the broader ecological influences that have a bearing on how these social experiences are formed, negotiated and managed. For this perspective, we need to look beyond children's digital play within clusters, towards the wider Preschool System (Table 2).

The Preschool System

In order to understand the dynamic nature of clusters, presented as part of the Digital Play System in the previous section, it is possible to draw on the Contextualist theoretical frame (Tudge 2008). From this perspective the multiplicity, and the often contradictory nature, of interactions and behaviours was partly informed by a series of broader ecological factors. That is to say that the negotiation processes in clusters were sensitively framed by the

Table 2. Children's engagement, interactions and behaviours as part of the Digital Play System.

Engagement	Interactions	Actions and Behaviours
Pro-social (Peer-Driven) Engagement – Children were focused predominantly on being involved with other children during the activity and observably contributed to the cluster	*Sociable Interactions* – The child attempts to have an extended interaction with other cluster members and may favour interaction with peers rather than with the technological resource	• Extended verbal exchange • Standing/sitting in close proximity to peers • Acknowledging or noticing other children by smiling or nodding • Verbally making their presence known • Verbal Invitation to play
	Sharing Interactions – The child allows their peers to use resources alongside them or instead of themselves	• Allowing others to control the technology (reqlinquishing control) • Offering and receiving objects
	Supportive Interactions – The child offers, receives or seek encouragement, urging the activity to continue	• Receiving approval or praise from a peer • Offering approval or praise to a peer • Seeking praise or attention
Anti-social Engagement – Children were focused on interacting as little as possible with peers and at times actively rejected any interactions	*Unsociable Interactions* – The child actively discards attempts by peers to interact in any form	• Ignoring others • Verbally rejecting invitations or help • Walking away
	Hostile Interactions – The child is violent and angry either verbally, physically or both	• Verbal abuse • Arguing • Misleading/'tricking' peers • Pushing
	Possessive Interactions – The child is reluctant to share the resource and makes every effort to be in sole control of the technology	• Taking objects followed by an altercation • Hiding/covering technology
Task-Driven Engagement – Focused on completing the task, which may include reaching the end of a level in a computer game, taking part in role-play with technologies or building a completed and functioning remote controlled car using Duplo Techs. The important thing, which distinguishes these interactions from others, was that task completion was the goal, irrespective of whether children were controlling the technology	*Helping Interactions* – children demonstrated or directed the child how to complete the task	• Demonstrating how to succeed/ Modelling • Physically Helping • Verbally directing • Listening to peers
	Exploratory/Investigatory Interactions – attempts to obtain knowledge	• Verbally Requesting Help • Q&A • Explaining • Observing task

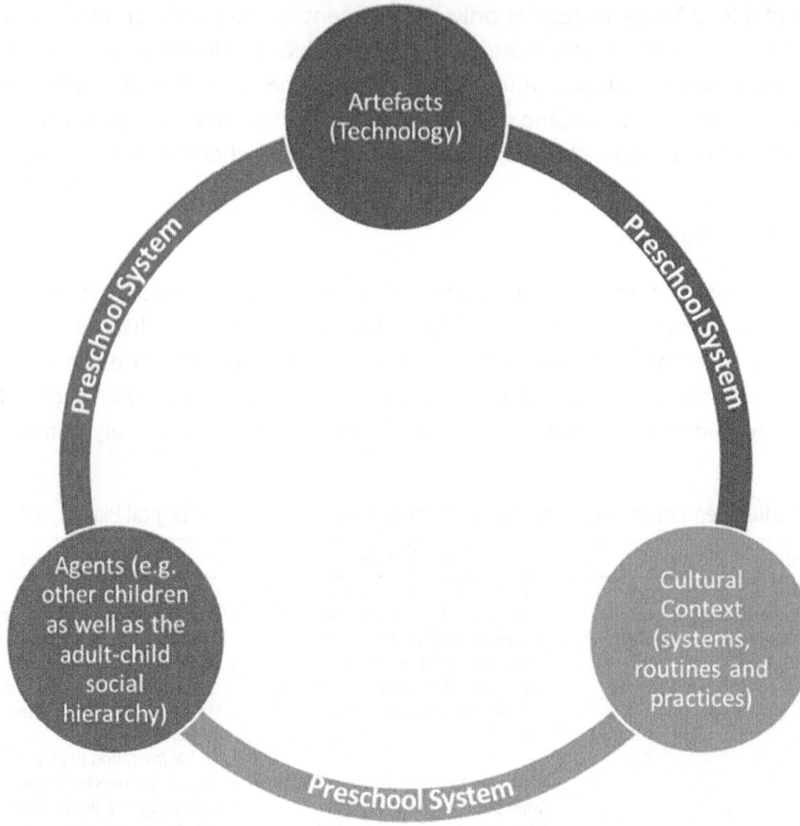

Figure 2. The Preschool System.

elements of the Preschool System: technological artefacts; cultural systems, routines and practices; and children and practitioners as social agents (shown in Figure 2).

Technological affordances and digital play

Findings from this study suggest that the affordances of technologies provided *opportunities* for children to interact in different ways during their digital play but did not determine the play episode. For example in some cases the physical properties of the technology were linked to the various technological positions that emerged. Importantly, in many cases, the affordances of the resource had both positive and negative influences for children's digital play. For example, the limited availability of resources in the playroom or the use of resources designed for individuals (such as desktop computers) encouraged children to share the resource and help their peers. Several instances of scaffolding and Guided Interaction (Plowman and Stephen 2007) were observed between peers when using technologies. In some cases, the increased challenge associated with the technological toys contributed to the need for scaffolding and helping interactions. For example, an experienced peer familiar with a game may demonstrate or explain to another child how to succeed as shown in the extract below:

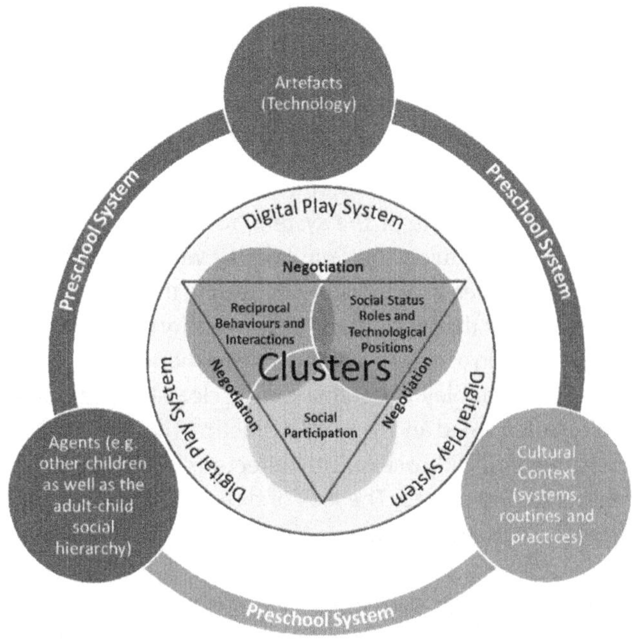

Figure 3. An ecological framework of children's social experiences during digital play.

> Grace begins to use the SMART board and Chris begins to use his finger to point at the screen to illustrate which selection she should choose as he verbally directs. Chris continues this process for each step of the way and Grace obeys. Then, when the game reaches a section where Grace does not need to make a selection and she needs to wait, he holds up his hand and says, "now wait". *(E50h Chris and Grace both age 4, SMART Board)*

Often the technologies required specific knowledge and skills that developed over time. As children reached the middle of the preschool year, those who regularly used the technologies quickly acquired this knowledge and skill and became expert users. Free choice in the playroom then allowed children to develop clusters as part of the Digital Play System and the combination of cluster development and children operating as experts provided *opportunities* for peer support and scaffolding. The helping interactions were often facilitated by the structure of the preschool culture, which encouraged turn-taking and sharing as part of the preschools' 'golden rules'.

On other occasions, the limited availability of technologies (for example, only one computer being available) or the affordance of 'isolate' resources (i.e. the computer being a personal device, or an individual mobile telephone) encouraged negative interactions and some children fought to gain access to the resource. Yet these instances were minimal and in most cases, children were skilfully able to manage and defuse the situation by referencing the rules and regulations embedded in the preschool context. There were few instances where practitioners had to step in to defuse the situation.

In the very brief examples above, it was possible to discern that varied interactions occurred around the same technologies, depending upon how the children negotiated the situation. In these cases, the affordances of the resource had a role to play in the development of digital play from a social perspective but they did not determine how the play experience would evolve. Indeed, technological affordances were only equally as influential as the cultural systems in place within the preschool and how children and practitioners operated as active agents in the system.

Systems, routines and practices in digital play

The Preschool System and culture contributed to the evolution of children's social experiences as they used their knowledge of the system, routines and predefined appropriate practice as reference points to guide their digital play when negotiating within clusters. Often children used technologies on their own, suggesting that potentially children's digital play is more 'free' than other activities. Yet, while the majority of observations in this project did not involve a practitioner in a proximal manner (Plowman and Stephen 2007), the distal influences on children's digital play were abundantly clear. Children operated within the confines of a system of well-framed and regulated practice. These settings were social places where practitioners, either implicitly or explicitly, directed children's behaviours, social interactions and how resources were used. The lack of direct involvement by practitioners did not therefore unburden children from the confines of the Preschool System during their digital play.

The system was facilitated by the ongoing development and reaffirmation of hierarchical power constructs, with adults and practitioners maintaining an authority that is absolute and unquestioned (Laupa 1994). Practitioners purposefully construct this power disparity, which contributes to children's everyday experiences, because it is through the construction of a system of mutually accepted practice, behaviours, routines and rules, that practitioners are comfortable 'affording' children freedom in their play. Thus, in order to give children agency in a world where practitioner accountability is high, practitioners first need to be confident that the children are both safe and capable of managing their own digital play experiences; they develop this confidence by instilling rules and routines.

In order to explain this, it is useful to draw on Bernstein's theory of Pedagogic Discourse. It became clear that inducting children into the rules and regulations of the preschool helps to create 'strong framing' through a strong 'regulative discourse' which creates a visible pedagogy for children to follow (Bernstein 2004). Bernstein argues that with a visible pedagogy, children are aware of the criteria of the discourse.

Nevertheless, children were not entirely devoid of agency, indeed they were able to experiment with the Preschool System, often pushing boundaries, reinterpreting or manipulating the structure. For many practitioners or on-lookers, the pushing of boundaries could be viewed as simple rule breaking, not understanding the rules or defying authority in a negative manner. Yet closer reflection on the data suggested that this process was a very sophisticated element of their negotiation processes within clusters during their digital play, and was not due to lack of understanding on the part of the children. In many cases, children were acutely aware of the expectations of behaviour, practice and play which afforded them the opportunity to find loopholes in the structure. Children, although aware of the adult rules, were able to negotiate their own culture and rules of social order. Thus, analysing the way children invoke or bend rules in the playroom helps to explore 'the cultural resources to which members orient in order to make sense of their social worlds' (Cobb-Moore, Danby, and Farrell 2009, 1478). This leads us to explore the role of children and practitioners as social agents.

Children and practitioners as social agents in digital play

Data collected in this study emphasise the role of the children and practitioners as social agents during digital play. The previous sections have talked extensively about how individuals within the social context shape their own, and others', digital play experiences. Children exhibited their agency in two ways.

(1) By assuming various social status roles and technological positions.
(2) By engaging in negotiation across and within clusters.

Similarly, practitioners exhibited their agency through the development of a system of routines, rules and regulations which are managed and maintained by constructing a power hierarchy between adults and children. Digital play is therefore influenced by the ways in which children and practitioners draw on the various technological affordances and the systems, routines and practices in the environment to make and shape decisions. Children and practitioners actively decide on a course of action in relation to these broader ecological factors, which culminates in their social experiences during digital play.

It was possible to see that children's decision-making within clusters had a considerable influence on their digital play experiences. Children actively sought out interactions with technologies, inviting others to join them in their play, offering help and feedback or just generally becoming a member of the cluster, for example. The decisions they made were informed by a series of interwoven elements. For example, increased challenges associated with technological artefacts at times encouraged requests for collaboration and help. Children were also able to use the cultural systems in place within the preschool as a reference to guide their interactions but equally, at times, they decided to circumvent or bend this system. Thus, their interactions were never consistent or predictable because the context in which they were playing was variable and inconsistent. Ultimately, children drew on the various interlinking elements that framed their digital play to decide on a course of action. Thus, it is clear that the two systems presented in the techno-ecological framework – the Digital Play System and The Preschool System – are interlinked.

An ecological framework of children's social experiences during digital play

The findings from this study offer a new perspective on children's digital play. When the two systems are combined, we are able to see their interdependence, which led to the techno-ecological framework presented in Figure 3.

Here we can see that children engage directly in the Digital Play System where they exhibit a variety of behaviours and degrees of social participation as well as assuming various technological positions and social status roles. All the while, the elements of The Preschool System – the technological affordances, the other agents in the preschool space and the cultural context – encircle children's play practices in the Digital Play System, subtly shaping, altering and framing the social experiences of children. Likewise, children's negotiation processes within the Digital Play System help The Preschool System to evolve. This relates to Stephen and Brown's (2004, 329) description of insiders who 'construct knowledge about the playroom as they participate in and, to some extent, shape that reality'.

It is not possible to attribute children's social experience and digital play to any one element of the framework in isolation. We need to understand that the ecology is a dynamic system in order to better understand how we can shape and facilitate high quality social and digital play experiences in preschools. This argument generates three important points to consider when trying to understand how technologies shape and contribute to early childhood practice.

(1) Technologies are not omnipotent, deterministic artefacts that direct, scaffold or 'teach' children, particularly in relation to social development and social experience.
(2) Children's digital play is complex but not entirely unique to other forms of play; particularly when technologies are integrated into children's experiences as part of well-established playful pedagogies and are utilised as tools within the play rather than the central play experience (Arnott 2016).
(3) Technologies form one element of a multifaceted and interconnected ecological preschool system. It is the interplay around The Preschool System, and across the Digital Play System, that results in observable social experiences during digital play.

From this, it is possible to say that practitioners need to carefully construct playful experiences in a manner that positions technologies as facilitating or contributory tools that may enhance the play, rather than viewing digital play as a central activity in itself.

Similarly, we need to consider that children draw on these various parts of the ecology as reference points in their play, which can lead to helpful negotiation processes during digital play. Literature on the structured nature of children's experiences in early childhood settings is widely available (Jordan, Cowan, and Roberts 1995). A paradox is often evident because early childhood education is portrayed, in theory, as a particularly child-led experience. In reality, however, children's lives are always rule bound, governed by adults in an authoritarian role and framed by a system of routines and 'appropriate practices' (Alcock 2007). As with many experiences in early childhood, it is the process which is fundamental to children's learning rather than the outcome of the digital play episode. This model demonstrates the factors which shape this process of negotiation and social experience and allows us to begin to understand how our agency, technologies and cultural context shape children's digital play. Not only can practitioners use this model to critically reflect on their own practice to inform planning but researchers are able to engage with the theoretical foundations which inform the framework to better decipher how children's play is evolving in the digital age.

References

Alcock, S. 2007. "Playing with Rules around Routines: Children Making Mealtimes Meaningful and Enjoyable." *Early Years* 27: 281–293.

Arnott, L. 2013. "Are We Allowed to Blink? Young Children's Leadership and Ownership While Mediating Interactions around Technologies." *International Journal of Early Years Education* 21: 97–115.

Arnott, L. 2016. "The Role of Digital Technologies." In *Early Years Foundation Stage: Theory and Practice*. 3rd ed., edited by I. Palaiologou, 329–342. London: Sage.

Bernstein, B. 2004. *The Structuring of Pedagogic Discourse*. London: Routledge.

Bers, M. U., and M. S. Horn. 2010. "Tangible Programming in Early Childhood." *High-tech Tots: Childhood in a Digital World* 49: 49–70.

Bird, J. Forthcoming. "Play-based Pedagogy: Children's Responses to Working and Non-working Technologies." In *Digital Technologies and Learning in the Early Years*, edited by L. Arnott. Sage.

Bird, J., and S. Edwards. 2014. "Children Learning to Use Technologies through Play: A Digital Play Framework." *British Journal of Educational Technology* 46 (6): 1149–1160

Broadhead, P. 2010. "Cooperative Play and Learning from Nursery to Year One." In *Play and Learning in the Early Years: From Research to Practice*, edited by L. Wood, P. Broadhead, and J. Howard, 43–60. London: Sage.

Bronfenbrenner, U. 1994. "Ecological Models of Human Development." *Readings on the Development of Children* 2: 37–43.

Bronfenbrenner, U. 1995. "Developmental Ecology through Space and Time: A Future Perspective." *Examining Lives in Context: Perspectives on the Ecology of Human Development* 619–647.

Brooker, L., and J. Siraj-Blatchford. 2002. "'Click on Miaow!' How Children of Three and Four Years Experience the Nursery Computer." *Contemporary Issues in Early Childhood* 3: 251–273.

Chandler, L. K., S. A. Fowler, and R. C. Lubeck. 1992. "An Analysis of the Effects of Multiple Setting Events on the Social Behavior of Preschool Children with Special Needs." *Journal of Applied Behavior Analysis* 25: 249–263.

Cobb-Moore, C., S. Danby, and A. Farrell. 2009. "Young Children as Rule Makers." *Journal of Pragmatics* 41: 1477–1492.

Cordes, C., and E. Miller. 2000. *Fool's Gold: A Critical at Computers in Childhood*. Maryland, MD: Alliance for Childhood.

Craft, A. 2012. "Childhood in a Digital Age: Creative Challenges for Educational Futures." *London Review of Education* 10: 173–190.

Creswell, J. W. 2012. *Qualitative Inquiry and Research Design: Choosing among Five Approaches*. London: Sage.

Driscoll, C., and M. Carter. 2009. "The Effects of Social and Isolate Toys on the Social Interaction of Preschool Children with Disabilities." *Journal of Developmental and Physical Disabilities* 21: 279–300.

Edwards, S. 2013. "Digital Play in the Early Years: A Contextual Response to the Problem of Integrating Technologies and Play-based Pedagogies in the Early Childhood Curriculum." *European Early Childhood Education Research Journal* 21: 199–212.

Fisher, J. 2008. *Starting from the Child: Teaching and Learning in the Foundation Stage*. Maidenhead: McGraw-Hill Education.

James, A., and A. James. 2004. *Constructing Childhood: Theory, Policy and Social Practice*. Basingstoke: Palgrave Macmillan.

Jordan, E., A. Cowan, and J. Roberts. 1995. "Knowing the Rules: Discursive Strategies in Young Children's Power Struggles." *Early Childhood Research Quarterly* 10: 339–358.

Laupa, M. 1994. ""Who's in Charge?" Preschool Children's Concepts of Authority." *Early Childhood Research Quarterly* 9: 1–17.

Livingstone, S., J. Marsh, L. Plowman, et al. 2015. *Young Children (0–8) and Digital Technology – UK Report*. Luxembourg: Publications Office of the European Union.

Ljung-Djärf, A. 2008. "The Owner, the Participant and the Spectator: Positions and Positioning in Peer Activity around the Computer in Pre-school 1." *Early Years* 28: 61–72.

Marsh, J. 2010. "Young Children's Play in Online Virtual Worlds." *Journal of Early Childhood Research* 8: 23–39.

Moyles, J. 2014. *The Excellence of Play*. Maidenhead: Open University Press.

Nolan, J., and M. McBride. 2014. "Beyond Gamification: Reconceptualizing Game-based Learning in Early Childhood Environments." *Information, Communication & Society* 17: 594–608.

Packer, M. J., and B. Scott. 1992. "The Hermeneutic Investigation of Peer Relations." In *Children's Development within Social Context. Research and Methodology*, edited by L. T. Winegar and J. Valsiner. Hillsdale, NJ: Lawrence Erlbaum.

Palaiologou, I. 2014. "Children under Five and Digital Technologies: Implications for Early Years Pedagogy." *European Early Childhood Education Research Journal* 24: 1–20.

Parten, M. B. 1932. "Social Participation among Pre-school Children." *The Journal of Abnormal and Social Psychology* 27: 243–269.

Parten, M. B. 1933. "Leadership among Preschool Children." *The Journal of Abnormal and Social Psychology* 27: 430–440.

Plowman, L. 2015. "Researching Young Children's Everyday Uses of Technology in the Family Home." *Interacting with Computers* 27: 36–46.

Plowman, L., and C. Stephen. 2007. "Guided Interaction in Pre-school Settings." *Journal of Computer Assisted Learning* 23: 14–26.

Plowman, L., O. Stevenson, C. Stephen, et al. 2012. "Preschool Children's Learning with Technology at Home." *Computers & Education* 59: 30–37.

Read, M. A., A. I. Sugawara, and J. A. Brandt. 1999. "Impact of Space and Color in the Physical Environment on Preschool Children's Cooperative Behavior." *Environment and Behavior* 31: 413–428.

Rogoff, B., J. Mistry, A. Göncü, and C. Mosier. 1993. "Guided Participation in Cultural Activity by Toddlers and Caregivers." *Monographs of the Society for Research in Child Development* 58: 1–179.

Rowan, C. 2015. *10 Reasons Why Handheld Devices Should Be Banned for Children under the Age of 12.* http://www.huffingtonpost.com/cris-rowan/10-reasons-why-handheld-devices-should-be-banned_b_4899218.html.

Rubin, K. H. 1977. "The Social and Cognitive Value of Preschool Toys and Activities." *Canadian Journal of Behavioural Science/Revue Canadienne Des Sciences Du Comportement* 9: 382–385.

SERA. 2005. *Scottish Educational Research Association Ethical Guidelines for Educational Research Scottish Educational Research Association.*

Shin, M. S., S. L. Recchia, S. Y. Lee, et al. 2004. "Understanding Early Childhood Leadership Emerging Competencies in the Context of Relationships." *Journal of Early Childhood Research* 2: 301–316.

Stephen, C., and S. Brown. 2004. "The Culture of Practice in Pre-school Provision: Outsider and Insider Perspectives." *Research Papers in Education* 19 (3): 323–344.

Strong-Wilson, T., and J. Ellis. 2007. "Children and Place: Reggio Emilia's Environment as Third Teacher." *Theory into Practice* 46: 40–47.

Tudge, J. 2008. *The Everyday Lives of Young Children: Culture, Class, and Child Rearing in Diverse Societies*. Cambridge: Cambridge University Press.

Tudge, J., L. Freitas, and F. Doucet. 2009. "The Transition to School: Reflections from a Contextualist Perspective." In *Educational Theories, Cultures and Learning: Critical Perspectives*, edited by H. Daniels, J. Porter, and H. Lauder, 117–133. London: Routledge.

Tudge, J. R. H., F. Doucet, D. Odero, T. M. Sperb, C. A. Piccinini, and R. S. Lopes. 2006. "A Window into Different Cultural Worlds: Young Children's Everyday Activities in the United States, Brazil, and Kenya." *Child Development* 77 (5): 1446–1469. doi:http://dx.doi.org/10.1111/j.1467-8624.2006.00947.

Vygotsky, L. S. 1978. *Mind in Society: The Development of Higher Psychological Processes*. Boston, MA: Harvard University Press.

Walmsley, D. J., and G. J. Lewis. 2014. *People and Environment: Behavioural Approaches in Human Geography*. Abingdon: Routledge.

Woods A. 2013. *Child-initiated Play and Learning: Planning for Possibilities in the Early Years*. Abingdon: Taylor & Francis.

Yelland, N. 2010. "New Technologies, Playful Experiences, and Multimodal Learning." In *High-tech Tots: Childhood in a Digital World*, edited by I. Berson and M. Berson, 5–22. Charlotte, NC: Information Age Publishing.

Digital play as a means to develop children's literacy and power in the Swedish preschool

Leif Marklund and Elza Dunkels

ABSTRACT

This paper presents different angles on the subject of digital play as a means to develop children's literacy and power, using an online ethnographical study of Swedish preschool teachers' discussions in informal online forums. Question posts ($n = 239$) were analysed using the Technological Pedagogical Knowledge framework and the Caring, Nurturing and Teaching framework, with the aim of understanding how teachers intended to support children's literacy development with tablets. Literacy development can be understood as a social practice that needs to develop along with changes in society's demands on citizens. The results presented indicate that school subject oriented skills are predominantly present in the mind-set of these preschool teachers. When digital play is increasingly used for pedagogical purposes in preschools, that also means that preschools have expanded their opportunities to work with children's literacy development. For preschool teachers, it is important to discuss how literacy development can be supported in a contemporary media landscape.

Background

In Sweden, many preschool teachers have the opportunity to let the children use tablets, if the preschool so chooses. A previous study of Swedish preschool teachers' use of online social network groups as informal professional development initiatives for discussing the educational use of tablets (Marklund, 2015) indicates that preschool teachers are developing their own understanding of how to approach digital play in preschools. In this article, 'learning' is incorporated into the concept of 'digital play', as play constitutes such an essential part of how teachers approach learning in Swedish preschools (Sheridan et al. 2011). Thus, 'literacy' is defined as a social practice that needs to develop along with changes in society. We thereby acknowledge the importance of letting children develop both traditional print literacy and the more multimodal aspects of literacy related to the concept 'digital literacy' (Gee 2012). Both these directions of literacy development are valid in the contemporary highly digitised Swedish society and in preparation for the increasingly, but not equally, digitised school context (Samuelsson 2014). The use of concepts like 'digital literacy' in educational discourse is a good example of how our understanding of literacy and literacy development needs to develop along with changes in society's demands on literacy. The transformation of literacy development practices and the introduction of IT in educational contexts are not straightforward tasks (Lindahl and Folkesson 2012) and, as the questions in the studied online discussions also indicated insecurities of different kinds regarding digital play, this paper aims to present different angles on the subject of digital play as a means of developing children's literacy and power.

According to the OECD (2014a), Sweden has one of the world's most developed IT infrastructures and one of the highest levels of Internet penetration. Fifty-nine per cent of the population have tablets in their homes, and 87% of families with children have several computers, smartphones and tablets (Findahl and Davidsson 2015). The same report reveals that about two-thirds of two-year olds have used the Internet and that about one-third use it on a daily basis. Children who attend Swedish preschools are between the age of one and six years old, and the attendance rates are higher than the OECD average (OECD 2014b), even though preschool is non-mandatory. These higher attendance rates could be explained by the moderate costs. Furthermore, the increased emphasis on the pedagogical aspects of the preschool makes parents value preschool as an important learning environment for their children (Statistics Sweden 2014). The Swedish preschool curriculum was revised in 2010, resulting in an increased emphasis on learning (Skolverket 2010). Furthermore, the use of IT has also become increasingly common since the launch of tablet technology on the Swedish market around 2010.

In this background section, we draw upon Lafton (2012), who presents a need to look beyond the idea of socially constructed knowledge building when analysing digital practices in preschools. She identifies three aspects making up a possible analytic space: individual knowledge; discourse and materiality. These three aspects constitute elements that affect how preschool teachers build, shape and construct their digital practices. Lafton argues that the lack of available training for preschool teachers in the educational use of digital technologies contributes to making the individual knowledge of preschool teachers a prerequisite for getting involved in digital practices. Further, she highlights how this personal digital knowledge seems to be different from preschool teachers' knowledge about topics like children's upbringing, play and learning. This existing body of socially constructed knowledge within preschool practice, and the fact that digital knowledge is, to a large extent, personal, could, according to Lafton (2012), be one reason why digital practices are sometimes looked upon as additions to early childhood education instead of being a natural part of the practice. Lafton also recognises that preschool teachers interpret their social setting as a group, and that the context surrounding this group has both social and material dimensions. The three dimensions: discourse; materiality and individual knowledge, form the structure of the following background.

Discourse

Ljung-Djärf (2004) argues that in order to understand an always, but sometimes slowly, changing preschool practice, it is important to recognise that preschool teachers need to position themselves and their practice in relation to discursive patterns in society. The concept of media panics (Drotner 1999) may inform this understanding. A media panic is an emotional, rather than rational, reaction to the introduction of new media. These reactions have caused a number of obstacles which preschools will have to overcome before they can fully involve digital play in their everyday activities. For instance, in 2011, the American Academy of Pediatrics recommended that parents should be informed about any screen media being used in children's education (Ernest et al. 2014). The risk discourse surrounding digital media has been in the foreground for at least two decades, so we may need a supplementary theory to explain the current risk perspectives. Kasperson et al. (1988) formulated the framework of social amplification of risk, stating that risk assessment is processed via scientists, media, individuals and groups of individuals, among others. To exemplify, Lafton (2012) found that preschool teachers seemed to have an unspoken understanding among themselves that games constitute an arena exclusively for children, which in practice led to adult absence when children were playing digital games.

Lindahl and Folkesson (2012) argue that the norms present within the Swedish curriculum can be used as an argument to resist as well as to welcome the introduction of IT in preschools. The various ways in which this is interpreted largely depend on what norms individual preschool teachers consider as prioritised but also on their views of children. For example, the view of children as competent may make preschool teachers prefer educational affordances which allow children to show their competencies without too much adult intervention. When, on the other hand, teachers feel a need to supervise and instruct children about the technology, this can give rise to conflict. Thus, this tension between norms in curricula and norms held by preschool teachers can constitute an obstacle to transforming preschool practice. For example, Ljung-Djärf (2004) found that most arguments for the use of IT in preschools were related to the future well-being of the children. She claims that our way of talking about the future and future society works as a discursive pattern. Thus, strong visions about IT in our society are present in the mind-set of preschool teachers, who are in a position to enable these visions to become reality within the preschool.

Furthermore, we found that research on discourse in relation to power and control may be useful. Thus, Lindahl and Folkesson (2012) suggest that preschool teachers should become more flexible regarding the degree of control in learning activities, and they argue that preschool teachers need to develop strategies to create open-ended learning activities and enhance their ability to observe and respond to children's initiatives. Howard, Miles, and Rees-Davies (2012) also support these results. They found that open questions create good conditions for play and learning. Correspondingly, Lynch and Redpath (2014) claim that closed apps position learners as consumers while open apps position learners as producers of knowledge. They point out that the use of more open apps helps create learning situations that resemble the more fluent way that IT is being used outside the formal school context. Moreover, Sandvik, Smørdal, and Østerud (2012) emphasise the importance of exploratory conversations when IT is being used in educational situations.

Karila and Rantavuori (2014) studied preschool and primary school teachers collaborating to create new practices to make the transition from preschool to school smoother for the children. They found that the primary teachers had more influence on how these lessons were designed. The preschool teachers' knowledge was to some extent marginalised in this collaboration. Their knowledge about play for pedagogical purposes was often neglected or left out of the discussions, which illustrates how school education is dominant in relation to early childhood and care traditions.

Materiality

It is not always easy to distinguish materiality from discourse, as Lynch and Redpath (2014) point out. They address the fact that IT has a long history of being described as an enabler of innovation and change, a notion that also has been supported by governmental discourse for decades, and that the institutionalised roles, structures and processes of schooling seem to work against implementing technologies in the classroom. The cause for this, according to Lynch and Redpath, is mainly that the introduction of IT is changing the roles and relations adopted in institutionalised ways of teaching and learning. Sandvik, Smørdal, and Østerud (2012) argue that children's interactions with tablets in preschool can be looked upon as literacy events or situations that make demands on children's literacy. They further argue that traditional print literacy is no longer enough to understand articulation and meaning-making in our society. In their view, communication should be regarded as being multimodal, in the sense that it is not possible to separate written text, images, sounds and numbers in a society that is increasingly dependent on the ability to read screens. As a way of resolving the division between digital and analogue, Edwards (2014) introduces 'contemporary play' as an important topic of discussion in early years education. She describes how the context of children's lives can currently be understood as a digital–consumerist context. In this new context, children are identified as a part of the consumer market and this seems to influence the conditions for child play. Instead of play during which adult life is interpreted, their play is in a digital–consumerist context characterised by 'the possibilities enabled by the convergence between various products, digital media and digital technologies across a continuum of digital to non-digital experiences' (224). With this perspective, changes in society might be the cause of changed patterns in children's play. And what potentially could be understood by early childhood educators as a decline in the quality of children's play, due to children's increased involvement with digital technologies, might in fact be new ways of playing, aligned with contemporary society but misaligned with our current conceptions of play and learning. However, Edwards (2014) emphasises that it is currently not known how these changed patterns of play affect children's development.

A less discursive-centred theme in current research deals with what features of apps are most important in the support of young children's learning. Falloon (2013) studied five-year-old children's interaction and learning with tablets and found some important qualities. Apps should communicate learning objectives in ways that young children can access and understand; provide smooth or distraction-free pathways towards achieving goals; include accessible and understandable instructions and teaching elements; incorporate formative corrective feedback; combine an appropriate blend of game, practice and learning components; and provide interaction parameters that are matched to the learning characteristics of the target student group. Both free and purchased apps were found to lack one or several of these important components, and therefore it is suggested that more research with this focus should be pursued in order to provide app developers with better knowledge about how to design apps that can support the literacy development of young children. In fact, Merchant (2015) claims that the lack of well-designed educational apps and a perhaps too strong belief in the intuitiveness of the technology are concerns for future research and development. Furthermore, Palmér (2015) found that the same teachers interacted differently with children depending on what kinds of apps were used. Different apps were also found to influence child participation and dialogue differently.

Gee (2012) claims that success in the school context is highly dependent on talk in children's homes because oral language is the foundation of any literacy learning. If this foundation is present in the lives of young children, it is of less importance if the mentoring is done relative to a book, media or a video game. If it is not present, both books and digital media can potentially become passive, in the sense that consumption does not develop knowledge and skills important for the future.

Individual knowledge

Sheridan et al.'s (2011) study aimed to uncover preschool teachers' thoughts in relation to teacher competence and the curriculum. It reveals three dimensions of how preschool teachers view what teacher competence entails: competence in knowing what and why, competence in know-how and interactive, relational and transactional competence. They also found that the participating teachers had broad multidisciplinary knowledge that needed to be enhanced in some areas, for example, when supporting learning in mathematics, science and when using IT. Most of the preschool teachers seemed willing to support children in developing knowledge in a wide range of areas, but social and ethical development was often considered more important than focusing on learning language and mathematics.

Teachers' positions are a frequent theme in current research on IT and learning in general. In a preschool setting, Merchant (2015) observed how teachers assisting children working with a story-app changed their position. Instead of posing questions or challenging the child regarding the story, they became more of a support concerning the tablet and app functionality. In fact, Merchant claims that studying tablet use may have 'the potential to reveal how power relations and uneven distribution of capital are instantiated in everyday encounters' (11). The issue of power is further discussed by Karila and Rantavuori (2014) who argue that it is important to learn more about the processes involved when transition practices are developed. Gee (2012) argues that individuals can reach two different levels of expertise in both traditional literacy and digital literacy. Developing a level of 'academic' language in relation to traditional literacy, reading or writing or a 'specialist/technical' language in relation to digital media or digital technologies is emphasised as being important for the individual in order to be able to achieve success in the modern world using these literacies. Furthermore, the meaning of teacher competence is something that is continuously being reconstructed in relation to changes in society and shifting values in guidelines and curricula for the preschool, according to Sheridan et al. (2011). They bring attention to how a new curriculum for the preschool (Skolverket 2010) and a new preschool teacher education were quite recently introduced in Sweden, factors that could affect the meaning teachers ascribe to teacher competence.

Howard, Miles, and Rees-Davies (2012) found that adult mediation in relation to computer use in preschool had a tendency to affect children's play experiences positively. The preschool teachers in their study were able to manage their interaction with the children in ways that supported the learning process while also providing the children with an appropriate level of autonomy, choice and control when playing and learning with the computers. Aubrey and Dahl (2014) point out the importance of adult mediation when IT is being used to support learning in early childhood settings. They claim that adults can play a role in enhancing children's thinking. Their study revealed, however, that neither parents nor early childhood educators had considered this as a conscious approach to enhance children's knowledge development in IT-related learning activities. Early childhood educators were also found to experience difficulties in determining an age-appropriate IT pedagogy. Bennett and Parise (2014) claim that our cultural practices have been computerised to a degree which will have future social consequences in our lives. They therefore argue that the results of technological advances should be integral parts of classroom activities. However, they also emphasise teachers' responsibility to make sure that the technology in question is introduced and used in a way which can develop the students' ability in critical reflection and make sure that what they learn will support them in their roles as citizens.

Sandvik, Smørdal, and Østerud (2012) argue that researchers and preschool teachers must work together to identify strategies for supporting learning with IT that will enable a balance between child-initiated and adult-led activities. They claim that the communicative role of the teacher and how the software is integrated in daily activities are relevant to the learning outcomes.

Purpose

The purpose of this study is to examine Swedish preschool teachers' online discussions regarding how they intend to use tablets and digital play in order to support children's literacy development.

Method

This study applied an online ethnographic method, inspired by netnography, a method that Kozinets (2010) claims can generate understanding of cultural phenomena. The aim was to provide insight into preschool teachers' intended literacy development practices using tablets and digital play.

Procedure

The Swedish equivalent of the word 'preschool' (förskola) was used to search within a commonly used online social network and a diversity of discussion groups about preschool-related subjects was found. Among these, two groups were strictly focused on discussing the educational use of tablets in preschool. Their similarities led to the decision to treat them as one set of data in this study.

Materials

The data consist of questions posed in two informal discussion groups for preschool teachers. At the time of data collection, the online discussions had been going on for a little less than two years and all posts initiating discussions were collected for further analysis. The posts collected for analysis ($n = 465$) consisted of questions ($n = 239$) and informative posts ($n = 226$). The present study focuses on a subset of the questions ($n = 151$) concerning either teaching-content related issues or pedagogical issues.

Participants

Together, these two discussion groups had 3386 participants (1320 + 2066) and the active participants had written 465 posts (240 + 225). The active participants who had initiated discussions with questions in these groups are to be considered as participants in this study. These participants should be considered as early adopters of technology and they are therefore not likely to be representative of the whole population of Swedish preschool teachers.

Ethical considerations

The study adheres to the ethical guidelines of the Swedish Scientific Council (Hemerén 2011), and the AoIR's guidelines on ethical issues (Markham and Buchanan 2012). The moderators of the discussion groups and the participants were informed about the nature of the study and the possibility to withdraw from it or have their posts excluded from the data-set. The moderators were contacted via direct messages and the participants via a message to each of the discussion groups, and no participants wanted their posts excluded. The information shared in these discussions was found to be non-sensitive and not potentially harmful to the participants.

Analysis

The participants' questions ($n = 239$) were first organised according to the Technological Pedagogical Content Knowledge framework (Koehler and Mishra 2009). This framework describes what kind of knowledge teachers need in order to teach efficiently with technology and the participants' questions were related to 'Technological Knowledge' ($n = 89$), 'Technological Content Knowledge' ($n = 76$) and 'Technological Pedagogical Knowledge' ($n = 75$). The questions that concerned content issues ($n = 76$) and pedagogical issues in relation to the technology ($n = 75$) revealed information about the preschool teachers' intended literacy development practices with tablets. Therefore, these questions ($n = 151$) were analysed using the following second framework.

Ljung-Djärf (2004) found that Swedish preschools have three different rationalities: caring, nurturing and teaching. Depending on how the preschool teachers drew upon these rationalities when using computers, the children ended up with different experiences of using computers in preschool. This second theoretical framework was used with the purpose of developing an understanding of:

- the intended ways to support children's literacy development with tablets,
- the rationalities preschool teachers draw upon when initiating discussions about tablets.

The framework of Ljung-Djärf (2004) provides information about what computer use would look like if preschool teachers drew on a caring, nurturing or teaching rationality in their work, respectively: what the content and aim of the learning activity would be, how the activity would be organised and what the learning environment would be like. In the present study, the questions did not provide information about how learning activities were organised, and the decision to assign a question to a specific rationality category of the framework was made according to the following aspects of Ljung-Djärf's (2004) rationalities:

- Caring rationality: The computer is considered as a leisure activity, where the main aims are having something to do and to practise taking turns. The computer is also considered a threat to other activities.
- Nurturing rationality: The computer is considered a nurturer, where the main aims are to stimulate responsibility, initiative and cooperation. The computer is also viewed as an available option among other activities.
- Teaching rationality: The computer is considered a tool for teaching and learning, where the main aims are to fulfil political visions and goals regarding equal conditions for learning. Computer use is also seen as an essential learning activity.

Each question was considered in relation to the described characteristics of the rationalities. The questions however rarely provided insight to all characteristics of the rationalities. Questions related to teaching content often provided information about the content and aim, the pedagogical intention to teach children certain content or skills using apps, which thereby led to the decision to assign them to the teaching rationality category. Pedagogically related questions were often placed into the framework based on the learning environment aspect of the rationality. For instance, most of these questions indicated that tablets were seen as an available pedagogical option among others, and therefore they were placed within the nurturing category. The remaining part of these pedagogical questions signalled that the preschool teachers had a critical or restrictive stance to perceived changes in their practice, and were therefore placed in the caring rationality category. Each of the rationality categories was thereafter analysed with a single step of thematic analysis (Clarke and Braun 2013) in order to find themes within these categories that could deepen our understanding of the intended literacy practices of tablets and digital play of Swedish preschool teachers.

Results

The following sections present how the preschool teachers' questions in the online discussions could be associated with a caring, nurturing or teaching rationality, drawing on the 'caring, nurturing, teaching' framework from Ljung-Djärf (2004). Each rationality contains themes that emerged in the data-set and the themes are exemplified with quotes.

Caring

A characteristic of caring rationality is to perceive contemporary media as a leisure activity and a threat to other activities (Ljung-Djärf 2004) and relatively few questions were placed within this category, probably because a majority of the preschool teachers in these discussions are in favour of introducing tablets in preschools and therefore do not consider tablets to be a threat to existing practices.

Convinced or reserved teachers and parents

The participants in these discussions have identified two groups of preschool teachers, those convinced about the benefits of using tablets in preschool and those who have reservations about introducing this technology in their practice, suggesting that some preschool teachers feel that aspects of their practice are threatened by the introduction of tablets.

> Hi! I will lead a course about tablets at the preschool where I work. Any suggestions on how I can 'convert' colleagues who are a bit sceptical when it comes to using tablets in preschool? To make them understand what a fantastic tool this really is!

In a similar post, a preschool teacher would like to be advised on how to approach parents who think that their children's learning environment is threatened.

> Hi! I work at a parent-led preschool and I would like to invest in a tablet. However, the parents are not convinced, so we need strong arguments.

The value of digital play

In some questions, traditional ways of supporting learning in preschool are being portrayed as threatened by the introduction of tablets.

> What can children learn using tablets that they cannot learn in other ways?

Concerns are also raised that teachers will become more passive when using tablets.

> My question to you is, how do you make sure that the tablet does not become a babysitter?

One preschool teacher responds to these discussions.

> I also have a reflection ... many of you seem afraid that the tablet will become a babysitter. In what respects are building-blocks a better babysitter then? Aren't all the pedagogical materials we have in preschools there to complement each other, the children are surely interested in different materials ... so why are we then so afraid that the tablet will become a babysitter if we are not present?

The same preschool teacher continues:

> I believe the problem is more related to our values and our way of perceiving technological development. If we are competent in our profession we will make our environment pedagogically diverse in a way which can support the development of our children!

Nurturing

A characteristic of nurturing rationality is to perceive the computer as an available option among others (Ljung-Djärf 2004) and a majority of the questions were placed within this category. The nurturing approach may be a consequence of these preschool teachers already being convinced about the educational value of tablets.

Apps as alternative pedagogy

These questions seem to be asked with the purpose of developing alternative pedagogical approaches, indicating that traditional learning activities might be presented to children in alternative ways.

> I'm looking for apps in which one may play theatre.

Apps as an enabler of pedagogy

The preschool teachers are also developing a use of tablets that enables new pedagogical affordances, for example, tablets are being used to support pedagogical work with children who speak another mother tongue or children who have special needs.

> Can anyone suggest apps in Spanish for children aged 3–4 years?

Insecurity among preschool teachers

Some preschool teachers seem insecure about how to approach tablets in their pedagogical work. This theme contains questions about overcoming this insecurity, along with questions aiming to reveal other colleagues' opinions and experiences of different apps.

> I am curious how you work with digital media in your preschool. How do you work pedagogically with IT together with the children, and what kind of digital media do you use?

Teaching

A characteristic of teaching rationality is to perceive the computer as a tool for teaching and learning and, according to Ljung-Djärf (2004), computer use is looked upon as an essential learning activity where the main aims are to fulfil political visions and goals regarding equal conditions for learning. Relatively few questions were placed in this category, largely due to the nature of the discussions in the online discussion groups, discussions during which the posts did not always provide detailed information about the aims of the activity. However, the questions placed in this category had a clear teaching aim and were focused on different teaching contents, which indicate that preschool teachers are interested in approaching tablets in various ways.

Intended literacy development

Most of these questions concern ways of supporting language development and children's literacy in the Swedish language, but also offer children a possibility to stay in contact with their mother tongue.

> I'm looking for good apps that can help develop the children's Swedish, both when it comes to articulation and understanding.

> I wonder if anyone may suggest any good apps in Arabic that we can use to stimulate mother tongue learning?

Some questions indicate a strong focus on the school readiness aspect of intended learning activities.

> I wonder if anyone may suggest good applications in mathematics, preferable geometry apps for ages 3–5 years.

Furthermore, we found questions regarding the use of tablets in outdoor education, music and drama as well as how to use tablets to develop children's collaborative skills and knowledge about feelings and empathy. In this respect, these preschool teachers seem open to a broad use of tablets, with varied learning objectives and diverse content.

Discussion

The purpose of this study was to examine Swedish preschool teachers' online discussions regarding how they intend to use tablets and digital play in order to support children's literacy development. The preschool teachers who participate in these discussions can be described as early adopters of educational technology. Jahnke and Kumar (2014) argue that it is important to research the initial understanding of teachers who are introducing tablets, as this may result in increased understanding among teachers who are hesitant about introducing tablets in their work.

Research on digital play in preschools may be said to have entered a second iteration of studies due to the introduction of tablet technology. In Sweden, digital play has previously been researched mainly in a computer context (Lindstrand 2015). The present study used these previous results to investigate whether tablets and computers are approached in different ways. Therefore, we used the caring, nurturing and teaching framework of Ljung-Djärf (2004) to examine how these rationalities were represented among the preschool teachers participating in online discussions about the educational use of tablets. Questions posed in these forums provided information about what learning activities the preschool teachers had planned to carry out with tablets. It thereby also became interesting to investigate what interpretations of literacy development were present in the mind-set of these preschool teachers.

The preschool teachers in our study discuss tablets and digital play with an emphasis on learning, and the discussions primarily concern language development or school-subject oriented knowledge and skills. The new Swedish preschool curriculum strongly emphasises learning in preparation for school. Thus, preschool teachers need to develop new ways of thinking about their practice (Jönsson, Sandell, and Tallberg-Broman 2012). In similar ways, the use of tablets could challenge preschool teachers to renegotiate certain aspects of their professional identity (Gee 2000; Marklund 2015). Traces of these parallel developments can be identified in the studied online discussions. At times, it seems as though questions might be related both to the new and stronger emphasis on the teaching role and to the insecurity associated with the introduction of tablets. Furthermore, the results of the present study indicate that there is a form of efficiency discourse among these teachers. They seem to use the support of colleagues to develop learning activities that fit the curriculum. They also use the discussions as a way to develop ways of working with tablets so that both preschool teachers and children will get the most out of this technology. Perhaps this is one reason why free play with tablets is rarely mentioned in the discussions.

In the discussions, it is also possible to identify insecurities regarding the teacher's role when tablets are used, and these questions often concern the degree of teacher presence needed when children use tablets. Some questions reveal that not all teachers know whether tablets should be treated like traditional materials that usually allow children more uncontrolled conditions to explore, play and learn. Studies confirm that these kinds of discussion are important, as preschool teachers' presence and ability to mediate the meaning-making process are important to the outcome of literacy events offered with the use of tablets (Aubrey and Dahl, 2014). From the online discussions, it is not possible to conclude how these preschool teachers arrange their pedagogical work with the tablets or how they interact with the children. However, other studies have shown a lack of awareness of the role of mediation among preschool teachers (Aubrey and Dahl, 2014; Lafton 2012). Nevertheless, the online discussions do indicate that many teachers are somewhat insecure about the affordances that tablets might bring. It is possible that this insecurity also concerns their ability to mediate and support meaning-making, as IT is known to change the adopted roles and relations within educational contexts (Lynch and Redpath 2014). In the discussions, there are only a few questions that directly address the mediator role. There are, however, quite a large number of questions where the preschool teachers seem to place a lot of trust in the inherent ability of educational apps to support children's literacy development. Perhaps this indicates a lack of awareness of their important role as mediators of meaning-making in tablet-supported learning activities. Howard, Miles, and Rees-Davies

(2012), Aubrey and Dahl (2014) and Bennett and Parise (2014), among others, stress that a mediator should use open instead of closed questions to help develop children's thinking. Some preschool teachers are concerned that IT might demand too much adult interference within a practice that in other respects wants to present an environment that children can manage by themselves (Lindahl and Folkesson 2012; Petersen 2015). However, Howard, Miles, and Rees-Davies's (2012) study indicates that children appreciate adult intervention in their digital play. Thus, preschool teachers may help improve literacy development among children who engage in digital play, if they decide to engage in dialogues with these children, instead of treating games as the children's own arena for actions (Gee 2012; Lafton 2012). Gee (2012) argues that interaction and mentoring in early life are the most influential factors for later success in literacy and content learning. Within the preschool environment, the teachers can take on a mediating role that can help overcome the reported shortcomings of current educational apps (Falloon 2013; Merchant 2015) and develop pedagogies that may enrich children's literacy development. Lindahl and Folkesson (2012) point towards the existence of such pedagogies regarding IT when they argue that preschool teachers need to develop strategies to create open-ended learning activities and to enhance their ability to observe and respond to children's initiatives.

The questions in the discussions reveal that the preschool teachers need feedback from colleagues regarding apps and what kind of apps might be suitable. This is confirmed by, among others, Aubrey and Dahl (2014) and Palmér (2015). Lantz-Andersson (2009) argues that technologies must be contextualised into the practice at hand and not the other way around. Even though many features of tablets seem well adjusted to preschools, tablets as such have not been developed with this educational practice in mind (Lantz-Andersson 2009). Sandvik, Smørdal, and Østerud (2012) claim that traditional print literacy is insufficient to understand articulation and meaning-making today. Therefore, they emphasise that children's interactions with tablets can be looked upon as vital literacy events. However, Marklund (2015) shows that preschool teachers often need to overcome barriers related to technology or materials when planning their learning activities.

Some questions express a need to discuss the value of digital play in preschools and how children can benefit from digital play. Samuelsson (2014) emphasises that Swedish children have different opportunities to develop digital literacies at home, which may be an argument for introducing tablets in preschool. The study also emphasises the fact that children in Swedish schools get different opportunities to get their digital literacies assessed in school. The latest statistics confirm that the use of the Internet to support children's learning in school varies a lot in Sweden, where some children use the Internet on a daily basis and some never use it for school work (Findahl and Davidsson 2015). Consequently, children face the risk that school will not see all aspects of their literacy as equally important, which in turn means that children might become differently empowered in the school context depending on which aspects of literacy they have developed during their early years. Janks (2010) argues that there will always be a dominant form of literacy within each secondary discourse that individuals enter, for example, when children progress from preschool to primary school. Awareness of how children's development of literacy correlates with the literacy demands of the next discourse that they will enter therefore seems important for preschool teachers to consider in relation to their use of tablets and digital play in preschools. The ways children's literacy development is supported will also influence children's opportunities to be successful, or powerful, when they enter the primary school context. Awareness about dominant forms of literacy is also, according to Janks (2010), a prerequisite for rethinking the literacy practices within a certain discourse or context, for example, how literacy development is supported and viewed in preschool. The present study indicates that tablets are, to a great extent, considered as one available pedagogical option among others or as a tool for teaching and learning. Support for language development and school-related knowledge seems to be present in the mind-set of these preschool teachers. If these findings are in fact representative of the literacy practices with tablets in Swedish preschools, tablets could arguably play a vital role in any effort to maintain the balance between education and care in Swedish preschools (Jönsson, Sandell, and Tallberg-Broman 2012). The ways that school education can be understood as dominant in relation to early childhood and care traditions (Karila and Rantavuori 2014) further contribute to the importance for preschool teachers of reflecting on the tendencies towards more school-oriented learning activities. In fact, this might partly be an outcome of this imbalanced power relation between school and preschool.

The results of this study show that there are two groups of preschool teachers in Sweden, those who are convinced about the affordances of tablets in preschools and those who remain reserved about the introduction of tablets in preschool. Lafton (2012) provides insight into how discourse is likely to affect the way preschool teachers approach tablets and digital play. Regarding discourse, we know how our beliefs about the future and ways of talking about it also work as a discursive pattern contributing to realising these beliefs (Ljung-Djärf 2004). Political and societal discourse about IT may find its way to the written curriculum, which ultimately preschool teachers will have the power to realise within their practice. The messages preschool teachers receive from the discourse about IT can be very different depending on what voices they decide to listen to. The amount of time children should be allowed to spend in front of screens is often at the forefront of discussions about children and media (Smahel et al. 2012). In the analysed questions, preschool teachers seek advice regarding how to position themselves relative to the variability of the information about tablets, information that may be associated with media panics (Drotner 1999). On the other hand, discourse can also work as a progressive force in relation to the use of IT in educational settings, for example when Skantz Åberg, Lantz-Andersson, and Pramling (2015) suggest a wider definition of what has historically been incorporated in the concept of text. Also, Sandvik, Smørdal, and Østerud (2012) argue that communication should be seen as multimodal. We would not like to take a stand against these claims; however, we would like to stress that even though the theoretical understanding of literacy and literacy development has expanded considerably due to the increased use of digital technologies, the power-related aspects of literacy development and literacy assessment in Swedish schools have not changed to the same degree (Samuelsson 2014). Preschool teachers therefore need to have a reflective stance regarding political, societal and media discourses in order to be able to develop ways of introducing tablets in the literacy development practices of preschools.

By applying the caring, nurturing and teaching analytic framework to the online discussion questions in our study, we found that preschool teachers draw on these rationalities in different ways in their approach to tablets, and in this respect, the results confirm the results of Ljung-Djärf (2004). The online discussions about tablets, however, indicate a concentration towards drawing on the nurturing and teaching rationalities, which might indicate an ongoing change regarding the pedagogical use of tablets in comparison to the more free-play oriented way that has previously been the approach to computers in Swedish preschools.

The preschool teachers in these online discussions, who are already convinced about the value of tablets in preschool, seem to be open to a broad application of the tablets within their practice. From the discussions, we understand that tablets are used for different types of educational contents and with different educational purposes. The results also show that these preschool teachers use tablets and digital play in order to create new learning opportunities, for example when it comes to the support of children who speak another mother tongue or to support children with special needs. However, even this group of early adopters of technology express concerns and insecurities. There seems to be a need for an increased understanding of both the experienced affordances and constraints of tablets as a means to support children's literacy development in Swedish preschools.

Concluding remarks

An important conclusion is that the pedagogically influential rationalities found by Ljung-Djärf (2004),caring, nurturing and teaching, are still found in the mind-set of Swedish preschool teachers when tablets are being introduced in their practice. Another conclusion is that the participants view tablets either as an available pedagogical option or as a tool for teaching and learning.

Being early adopters of educational technology, this group cannot serve as representatives of preschool teachers in Sweden. We argue that it is important for hesitant preschool teachers to consider the contemporary context of children's play and learning (Edwards 2014) and how digital technologies are an integral part of contemporary life (Findahl and Davidsson 2015). Also, we may continue to discuss whether and how tablets and digital play can be used appropriately in the contexts of preschools, with the purpose of enhancing the literacy and power of each individual child. We believe that a literacy and power perspective, where the literacy affordances of the contemporary media landscape are emphasised, can work as a fruitful middle ground between hesitant and progressive preschool teachers when digital play is being discussed in preschools.

Disclosure statement

No potential conflict of interest was reported by the authors.

ORCID

Leif Marklund http://orcid.org/0000-0003-3856-1519
Elza Dunkels http://orcid.org/0000-0003-2673-1808

References

Aubrey, C., and S. Dahl. 2014. "The confidence and competence in information and communication technologies of practitioners, parents and young children in the Early Years Foundation Stage." *Early Years* 34 (1): 94–108.

Bennett, M., and M. Parise. 2014. "Computer Technology: Possibilities and Pitfalls." *Childhood Education* 90 (5): 365–369.

Clarke, V., and V. Braun. 2013. "Teaching Thematic Analysis." *Psychologist* 26 (2): 120–123.

Drotner, K. 1999. "Dangerous Media? Panic Discourses and Dilemmas of Modernity." *Paedagogica Historica* 35 (3): 593–619.

Edwards, S. 2014. "Towards Contemporary Play: Sociocultural Theory and the Digital-consumerist Context." *Journal of Early Childhood Research* 12 (3): 219–233.

Ernest, J. M., C. Causey, A. B. Newton, K. Sharkins, J. Summerlin, and N. Albaiz. 2014. "Extending the Global Dialogue about Media, Technology, Screen Time, and Young Children." *Childhood Education* 90 (3): 182–191.

Falloon, G. 2013. "Young Students Using iPads: App Design and Content Influences on Their Learning Pathways." *Computers & Education* 68: 505–521.

Findahl, O., and P. Davidsson, 2015. *Swedes and the Internet*. [online]. Accessed December 1, 2015. http://www.soi2015.se/the-swedes-and-the-internet-2015-summary/

Gee, J. P. 2000. "Identity as an Analytic Lens for Research in Education." *Review of Research in Education* 25: 99–125.

Gee, J. P. 2012. "The Old and the New in the New Digital Literacies." *The Educational Forum* 76 (4): 418–420.

Hemerén, G. 2011. *God forskningssed* [Research guidelines from the Swedish Research Council]. Stockholm: Vetenskapsrådet.

Howard, J., G. E. Miles, and L. Rees-Davies. 2012. "Computer Use within a Play-based Early Years Curriculum." *International Journal of Early Years Education* 20 (2): 175–189.

Jahnke, I., and S. Kumar 2014. "Digital Didactical Designs : Teachers' Integration of iPads for Learning-centered Processes." *Journal of Digital Learning in Teacher Education* 30 (3): 81–88.

Janks, H. 2010. *Literacy and Power*. London: Routledge.

Jönsson, I., A. Sandell, and I. Tallberg-Broman. 2012. "Change or Paradigm Shift in the Swedish Preschool?" *Sociologia, Problemas E Praticas* 69: 47–61.

Karila, K., and L. Rantavuori. 2014. "Discourses at the Boundary Spaces: Developing a Fluent Transition from Preschool to School." *Early Years* 34 (4): 377–391.

Kasperson, R. E., O. Renn, P. Slovic, H. S. Brown, J. Emel, R. Goble, Jeanne X. Kasperson, and S. Ratick. 1988. "The Social Amplification of Risk: A Conceptual Framework." *Risk Analysis* 8 (2): 177–187.

Koehler, M. J., and P. Mishra. 2009. "What is Technological Pedagogical Content Knowledge?" *Contemporary Issues in Technology and Teacher Education* 9 (1): 60–70.

Kozinets, R. V. 2010. *Netnography : Doing Ethnographic Research Online*. Los Angeles, CA: Sage.

Lafton, T. 2012. "How Early Childhood Practitioners Build, Shape, and Construct Their Digital Practices: The Search for an Analytical Space." *Nordic Journal of Digital Literacy* 7 (3): 172–186.

Lantz-Andersson, A., 2009. "Framing in Educational Practices. Learning Activity, Digital Technology and the Logic of Situated Action." Dissertation in Education (No.278). University of Gothenburg, Göteborg.

Lindahl, M. G., and A.-M. Folkesson. 2012. "ICT in Preschool: Friend or Foe? The Significance of Norms in a Changing Practice." *International Journal of Early Years Education* 20 (4): 422–436.

Lindstrand, S. H. 2015. "Are We Spinning or Is It The Board? – Young Children's Interaction with an Interactive Whiteboard In Preschool." *Nordic Journal of Digital Literacy* (03), 124–144.

Ljung-Djärf, A. 2004. "Spelet runt datorn: datoranvändande som meningsskapande praktik i förskolan." [The Game around the Computer: Computer Use as a Meaning Making Practice in Preschool.] Dissertation in Education (No.12). Malmö : Lärarutbildningen, Malmö högsk.

Lynch, J., and T. Redpath. 2014. "'Smart' Technologies in Early Years Literacy Education: A Meta-Narrative of Paradigmatic Tensions in IPad Use in an Australian Preparatory Classroom." *Journal of Early Childhood Literacy* 14 (2): 147–174.

Markham, A., and Buchanan, E., 2012. *Ethical Decision-Making and Internet Research – Recommentations from the AoIR Ethics Working Committee* (Version 2.0). Accessed February 17, 2015. http://aoir.org/reports/ethics.2.pdf

Marklund, L. 2015. "Preschool Teachers' Informal Online Professional Development in Relation to Educational Use of Tablets in Swedish Preschools." *Professional Development in Education* 41 (2): 236–253.

Merchant, G. 2015. "Keep Taking the Tablets: iPads, Story Apps and Early Literacy." *Australian Journal of Language & Literacy* 38 (1): 3–11.

OECD (Organisation for Economic Co-operation and Development). 2014a. *Broadband and Telecom, OECD Broadband Statistics Uptade* [Online]. Accessed December 1, 2015. http://www.oecd.org/internet/broadband/broadband-statistics-update.htm

OECD (Organisation for Economic Co-operation and Development). 2014b. *Sweden: Education at a Glance 2014: Country Note*. [Online]. Accessed December 1, 2015. http://www.oecd.org/edu/Sweden-EAG2014-Country-Note.pdf

Palmér, H. 2015. "Using Tablet Computers in Preschool: How Does the Design of Applications Influence Participation, Interaction and Dialogues?" *International Journal of Early Years Education* 23 (4): 365–381.

Petersen, P. 2015. "'That's How Much I Can Do!' – Children's Agency in Digital Tablet Activities in A Swedish Preschool Environment." *Nordic Journal of Digital Literacy* 9 (3): 145–169.

Samuelsson, U. 2014. "Digital (in)Equality? ICT Use in School and Pupils Technological Capital." Dissertation in Education (No.23). Jönköping University, Jönköping.

Sandvik, M., O. Smørdal, and S. Østerud. 2012. "Exploring iPads in Practitioners' Repertoires for Language Learning and Literacy Practices in Kindergarten." *Nordic Journal of Digital Literacy* 2012 (3): 204–220.

Sheridan, S., P. Williams, A. Sandberg, and T. Vuorinen. 2011. "Preschool Teaching in Sweden – A Profession in Change." *Educational Research* 53 (4): 415–437.

Skantz Åberg, E., Lantz-Andersson, A., and Pramling, P., 2015. "Children's Digital Storymaking – The Negotiated Nature of Instructional Literacy Events." *Nordic Journal of Digital Literacy* (03), 170–189.

Skolverket. 2010. *Curriculum for the Preschool Lpfö 98, Revised 2010*. Stockholm: Skolverket.

Smahel, D., Helsper, E., Green, L., Kalmus, V., Blinka, L., and Ólafsson, K., 2012. *Excessive Internet Use among European Children*. EU Kids Online report. London School of Economics. [online]. Accessed December 1, 2015. http://eprints.lse.ac.uk/47344/1/Excessive%20internet%20use.pdf

Statistics Sweden. 2014. *De flesta barn i förskola – oavsett bakgrund* [Most Children Attend Preschool – Regardless of their Background]. [online]. Accessed December 1, 2015. http://www.scb.se/sv_/Hitta-statistik/Artiklar/De-flesta-barn-i-forskola–oavsett-bakgrund/

Teachers' dispositions towards the role of digital devices in play-based pedagogy in early childhood education

Ioanna Palaiologou

ABSTRACT
A body of research is emerging on early childhood education teachers' views on the integration of digital technologies in their practice. Despite evidence of the digitalisation of homes in affluent societies and children's interactions in highly mediated digital environments, few teachers so far have integrated digital devices into a play-based pedagogy. Thus, this project aimed to examine the attitudes and aptitudes towards digital devices of teachers in their personal lives and professional practice in five countries (England, Luxemburg, Malta, Greece and Kuwait). An online survey designed to collect broad-scale data was followed by focus group interviews. The findings demonstrated that although teachers are digitally competent in their personal lives, there is a dominant ideology regarding the nature of play-based pedagogy that hinders the integration of digital devices into their practice.

Introduction

The term 'digital devices' is used here as a collective term for all equipment that contains a computer or microcontroller and to which adults and children might have access, a list which now includes toys, games consoles, digital cameras, media players and smartphones as well as handheld, laptop or desktop computers. Research into early childhood education (ECE) in recent years has been concerned with the use of digital devices both at home and at school. Emergent evidence illustrates that many children inhabit high specification technological home environments where digital devices are part of their lives (Holloway, Green, and Livingstone 2013; Kalas 2010; Ólafsson, Livingstone, and Haddon 2014; Plowman and McPake 2013). Findings suggest that children use a range of devices from a very young age and that their digital imprint begins from birth. Studies from around the world (Fleer 2013a; Marsh et al. 2005; Plowman 2015; Terreni 2011), and cross-national comparisons (Chaurdon 2015; Livingstone et al. 2015; Palaiologou 2014; Rideout, Foehr, and Roberts 2010; Wartella 2013) have illustrated that many children grow up in technologically rich homes and are interacting with digital devices daily which parents see as positive, although some researchers express concerns about the online use of such devices. Research also examines how digital devices can support children's learning (Falloon 2013) for instance of literacy (Gonzalez and Fryer 2012; Marsh 2012;Nash 2012), arts (Terreni 2011) and maths (Jowett, Moore, and Anderson 2012), concluding that they 'may offer an exciting platform for consuming and creating content in a collaborative, interactive way' (Melhuish and Falloon 2010, 1).

Other research examines teachers' views and competencies and the opportunities for integrating digital devices into a play-based pedagogy (Hatzigianni and Margetts 2012; Inan and Lowther 2010; Kerckaert, Ruben Vanderlinde, and van Braak 2015; Nikolopoulou and Gialamas 2015a; 2015b). These studies conclude that, compared to primary and secondary education, the integration of digital devices into ECE has been slow and limited. Consequently, although children are interacting with digital devices from infancy and even have experiences at home with the Internet (Teuwens 2011), discussions about how digital devices can be integrated have not fully developed and there is evidence of concern that they might harm a play-based pedagogy (Lindahl and Folkesson 2012a, 2012b; Morgan 2010; Plowman and Stephen 2005). It is important, therefore, to examine what is meant by play-based pedagogy in early childhood and the factors that may influence the integration of digital technologies into ECE.

'Play-based Pedagogy' and 'Digital-play' pedagogical practices

In the field of ECE, play and pedagogy are two constructs that have informed recommendations for a learning environment for children that should be based on exploration, creativity, imagination, motion and emotions that integrate play in daily practices in ways that align with planned outcomes (Dahlberg and Bloch 2006; Hedges and Cullen 2011; Taguchi 2010; Wood 2014). Play-based pedagogy is based on the ideology that play has motor, spatial, cognitive, emotional, social and moral values in children's development and is dependent on the idea of an active child who engages in actions that will lead to deep understanding and meaning making experiences. Pedagogical practices in ECE derive inspiration from practices that value 'embodied hands-on experience based teaching and learning, often using aesthetic means of expression as a way [for children] to learn differently' (Taguchi 2010, 23). Central to a play-based pedagogy is the assertion that 'these activities are imbued with children's concerns with agency, power and self-actualisation, as well as their motivations to learn' (Wood 2014, 154). Research suggests, however, that perspectives and practices in relation to play and digital devices in ECE show a schism between researchers and teachers (Edwards 2013; Marsh and Bishop 2014; Verenikina and Kervin 2011; Wood et al. 2008). Despite the technologically rich homes of children, there are still concerns as to whether digital devices have a place in ECE (Howard, Miles, and Rees-Davies 2012; Yelland 2011) and about their inadequate integration into practice (Parette and Blum 2013).

There has been relatively limited examination to date of children's interactions with digital devices in ECE. The research that emerges either examines the extent to which children's interactions with digital devices can be characterised as play (Verenikina and Kervin 2011), or is concerned with comparisons of traditional vs. technological play (Bergen 2012). Such research defines play via a stereotypical ideology where children choose from a range of materials or activities in order to create experiences for meaning making. The relationship between play and digital devices has been limited in investigations, however, by a lack of clarity as to what the purpose of children's play is and what interactions can be seen as play.

Edwards (2013, 204) opposes the separation of play and digital devices, arguing that

> addressing the gap between play and technologies in early childhood curricula requires a perspective that helps teachers see how children's digital play supports their cultural meaning making, not further research that tells them how digital play compares to traditional play.

In other words, we need to make digital devices available as tools that extend possibilities for children as part of their play.

Factors affecting the integration of digital technologies in ECE

Research is emerging on teachers' views and attitudes towards the integration of digital devices (Aldhafeeri, Palaiologou, and Folorunsho 2016; Inan and Lowther 2010; Kerckaert, Ruben Vanderlinde, and van Braak 2015; Morgan 2010; Nikolopoulou and Gialamas 2015a; Sang et al. 2010; Teuwens 2011). Examination of these findings indicates that three conditions affect the integration of digital devices into ECE practice: teachers' agency; the ambiguities of play-based pedagogy ideology; and concerns for the dominance of materiality and for children's safety and well-being.

(1) Teachers' agency

Research suggests that teacher beliefs, digital capabilities and capacity to conceptualise how digital devices can be integrated shape their receptiveness towards them. There is a belief that digital devices harm child-centred pedagogy (Morgan 2010), prevent and limit children's physical activity (Cordes and Miller 2000) and lead to emotional and social isolation. Levin and Wadmany (2008) further suggest that technology adaptation requires a cognitive transformation in teacher beliefs. In that sense, transforming practice is a complex task (Mills and Tincher 2003) as it 'shapes practitioners' [teachers'] tacit theories-in-action in ways that compete with or override ideas encountered in initial or continuing professional education' (Stephen 2010, 19). Transformation is further prevented by lack of resources and poor planning (Smerdon et al. 2000), inadequate training (Aubrey and Dahl 2014) and teachers' experience in education (Hermans et al. 2008).

(2) The ambiguities of play-based pedagogy ideology

Researchers have argued that the notion of play is poorly articulated (BERA ECE SIG 2003; Moyles, Adams, and Musgrove 2002; Stephen 2010; Wood 2014) and that a play-based pedagogy is associated with first-hand experiences rather than 'a set of contextualised practices that are constantly adapting to circumstances' (Beetham and Sharpe 2007, 6). Instead of agonising about whether technologies can be included in a play-based pedagogy, ECE should deconstruct the characteristics of play and seek an evidence-based rationale. It is time for critical empirical and theoretical investigation of the contribution of digital devices in children's play and the opportunities offered for children to experiment with meanings. It is also time to move away from asserting relationships between play and digital technologies, questioning the efficacy of digital technologies in play-based pedagogy, and, instead, to offer technological continuity between home and school (Bittman et al. 2011; Edwards 2013; Marsh 2010; Plowman, McPake, and Stephen 2008).

(3) Concerns about the dominance of materiality, and about children's safety and well-being

> There is a view that digital devices are objects that require a material framework and that such a framework has transformed their potential effects on young children (Alliance for Childhood 2004; Palmer 2006, 2008; Sewlyn 2011). Critics of digital technologies view them as having a negative impact on children's safety, health and well-being (Kabali et al. 2015; Radesky et al. 2015) and distracting children's attention from educational content (Roseberry et al. 2014). Studies examining the use of digital devices in relation to socio-economic status, parents' education status and personality traits claim that these devices are used as a 'shut up toy' during parental daily routines (Radesky et al. 2014) with detrimental consequences for children's later social-emotional outcomes. Finally, it is suggested that interactions with technologies may affect children's development by replacing interactions with parents, carers or teachers (Kirkorian et al. 2009).

The factors influencing the integration of digital devices in ECE include external aspects such as resources and training and internal factors such as beliefs and views. This has led to 'a dualism where problems and benefits are pitched against each other' (Fleer 2013a, 57) and play-based pedagogy is separated from children's digital interactions, undermining the integration of digital technologies into ECE (Bittman et al. 2011 and Falloon 2013; Fleer 2011, 2013b). Research cautions us to focus on working 'towards the common goal of increasing children's digital autonomy and critical thinking for a safe and balanced life' (Chaudron 2015, 29) in order to 'bridge the gap between play and technologies' (Edwards 2013, 209).

Central to this is the role of teachers in terms of beliefs, feelings and behaviours towards digital devices (attitudes) as well as their capacity to use digital devices (aptitudes) and their dispositions. Thus, the research reported in this study aimed to examine teachers' attitudes and aptitudes in order to investigate what dispositions teachers exhibit towards the integration of digital devices in play-based pedagogy.

Theoretical underpinning of the study

Attitudes and aptitudes affect how we make sense of children's interactions with digital devices and therefore give direction to our behaviours, motives and intentions and consequently inform our dispositions and responses. Hence, a synergy between attribution theory and attitude theory from social psychology underpins this study in order to examine teachers' attitudes and aptitudes in relation to digital devices in ECE. This study considers how human actions, interactions, motives and intentions are shaped by the perceptions of a certain situation, and how attitudes and aptitudes offer meaning and direction based on personal experience, providing frames of reference which influence individuals' responses and dispositions towards a phenomenon or situation.

The study was guided by Weiner (1986) attributional theory of motivation, Schachter's (1964) cognitive labelling theory, Bem's (1972) self-perception theory, Katz's (1960) four functions of attitudes and Stahlberg and Frey's (1988) three component views of attitudes. Following their ideas for tracking the causes of human behaviour, the project aimed to move beyond teachers' views and focus on their attitudes and aptitudes – positive or negative – as an indicative and evaluative way of examining emotional and cognitive dispositions towards the integration of digital technologies in ECE.

Research context

The study utilised an online survey followed by focus group interviews across five countries: Greece, Malta, England, Kuwait and Luxemburg. In two previous studies (Aldhafeeri and Palaiologou 2016; Aldhafeeri, Palaiologou, and Folorunsho 2016; Palaiologou 2016), these countries were studied in relation to children's access to digital technologies at home. Since the completion of these projects, links were developed with these countries which allowed us to carry out the current project. As these countries have different languages, the challenge in this project could have risen from translation issues, but this difficulty was minimised because the languages were all in the repertoire of languages of the research team. The countries also offer an interesting comparison on the basis of the extent to which they have been digitalised. Kuwait, England and Luxemburg have introduced near universal digitalisation whilst Greece and Malta have only recently introduced the digitalisation of services.

In the first stage of research, an online survey was developed with the data collected used to identify any similar or different themes in teachers' responses. This was followed by focus group interviews. This mixed methods design was considered appropriate as the first stage generated themes across all countries which informed the focus groups. The EECERA code of ethics (2014) was followed throughout.

Stage 1: online survey

The survey developed around two key elements of the investigation – the attitudes and aptitudes of teachers and their views on two aspects of play: what children's behaviours they associate with play, and what they understand by play-based pedagogy. 'Attitudes' concerned teachers' beliefs, feelings and actions towards digital devices whilst 'Aptitudes' focused on their capacity to integrate digital devices into their personal and work life. Although in psychological studies scales are used to examine a person's attitudes and aptitudes, the intention in this research was not to provide direct or indirect measurements. Instead the intention was to investigate teachers' perceptions of their familiarity with digital devices. Thus, this part of the survey was developed around three key themes:

(1) *Task-behavioural orientation* aimed to collect data about tasks they undertake in their personal and work life using digital devices (19 items).
(2) *Emotional orientation* which aimed to collect feelings towards digital devices in their personal and work lives (28 items).
(3) *Coping orientation* focused on their intentions when using digital devices in their personal and work life (25 items).

The second part of the survey asked teachers to rate items of behaviours they associate with play when children are participating in activities such as symbolic play, role play and play with digital devices (17 items). It also asked them to rate statements associated with play-based pedagogy (13 statements).

The online survey was piloted three times in each country. It was developed firstly in English and then translated by the research team in the other countries so all the participants were presented with the questionnaire at all stages (piloting and main phase of research) in their own language. The Fundamental Lexical Hypothesis (FLH) technique was used in the design of the questionnaire in order to limit the translation effect in the survey (Barrett and Kline 1982; Cattell 1973). This technique offers researchers the opportunity to develop items that are related to individuals' beliefs, feelings and perceptions and express them linguistically and eventually to encode them into their own language. Although FLH encodes personality characteristics in single words, in this research the development of the statements was not limited to single words, but FLH was used as a technique to develop statements that would correspond in all languages.

For ethical reasons, descriptive statistics were used as they are accessible to inexperienced researchers, meaning the results could be communicated to all participants.

All participants in the project were recruited from lists provided by the responsible Ministry for ECE. An email was sent to the teachers in each country in their own language asking them whether they were willing to participate in the online survey and the sample was chosen from the responders. The survey intended to capture the views of teachers who were relatively new to the profession, but who also had some work experience. In keeping with standard procedures in cross-country comparisons, the same number of responses were analysed (184 teachers from each country who had worked between 5 and 10 years in ECE and were working with children from the age of 2–4 years), a total population of 920 participants. The average age of the teachers was 25–30 (73.7%) with the exception of England, where the average age was 20–25 (71.6%). Only 9.4% of the overall population were graduates and 32.4% were enrolled in a university course. All participants are referred to as teachers, although the majority do not have graduate status, since all are working in ECE and are responsible for delivering educational activities.

Quantitative results

In terms of attitudes towards digital devices in their personal life teachers showed a high level of approval across all countries (73.21%) with few disapproving of them (14.7%). The most common digital devices were iPhones (56.3%), smartphones (52.1%) and tablets (54.3%). Favourite activities were listening to music with a digital device (65.4%), watching TV (87.6%) and using social media (72.6%). Data showed consistency in terms of teachers' personal attitudes with no significant differences between countries.

The picture was similar for aptitudes in the use of digital devices in their personal lives and showed high levels of competence with digital devices (72.4%). High levels of confidence were also exhibited (64.4%); as well as coping strategies when faced with a problem with a digital device (72.1%) or with changing digital devices (63.2%). Again there were no statistically significant differences among teachers' aptitudes between the countries.

The picture was different, however, when it came to their practice in ECE where levels of attitudes and aptitudes towards digital devices dropped across all countries (with only Luxemburg showing a slightly higher percentage of positive attitudes towards digital devices in their practice >4.7%). Although teachers indicated they had the ability and willingness to learn new skills required in their teaching in relation to digital devices (73.2%), they felt unprepared to handle them in their classroom (65.4%), unsure about how they facilitate children's play (57.3%), confused about how they can be embedded in their practice and concerned about how they could recognise children's play behaviours and reactions when interacting with technologies (64.3%).

Teachers associated play with children's activities (83.2%), exploring materials (71.3%), socialising (83.2%), experiencing materials (92%), playing outside (82.3%) and self-chosen activities (73%). A large majority of teachers felt confident that they recognised playful characteristics when children are engaging with activities (92%). Table 1 illustrates their association of play behaviours with digital devices in comparison with other activities.

As can be seen all items have been associated with play for other activities, but when it comes to children's interactions with digital devices the percentages are lower. Teachers thus seem to have an understanding of play as being the result of engagement in activities that are related with spontaneity (98%), pleasure (96.3%) and motor (70.1%), spatial (93.2%), emotional (76.4%), social (67.8%) and cognitive (87.4%) experiences.

Table 2 illustrates teachers' views on play-based pedagogy and whether they think digital devices can become part of it. The table presents the collective results among all countries as there were no statistically significant differences. The statements used in this part of the survey were to investigate a potential definition of play-based pedagogy that was not coming from an academic-oriented terminology, and also any features of the digital devices which contributed to a play-based pedagogy.

The findings demonstrated that although teachers have attitudes and aptitudes which would enable them to integrate digital devices in their lives, they are hesitant about integrating these in their practice. Thus, focus groups were undertaken to gain an understanding of this difference.

Table 1. Teachers responses (%) on whether children exhibit playful behaviours when they interact with digital devices (n = 920).

Do you recognise the following as behaviours of play when children	Engage with activities on their own	Engage with activities with peers	Engage with planned activities by an adult	Engage with planned activities by another child	Engage with digital devices
Self-chosen interactions	86	65.4	54	28.4	21.1
Self-inspired interactions	65.3	46.6	31.6	22.1	14.5
Self-regulated interactions	38.2	46.7	29.8	45.6	7.1
Children are inventive	83.1	50.1	21.4	23.8	6.3
Children are creative	76.3	50.5	43.2	52.6	8.4
Children are motivated	69.3	50.1	43.6	38.9	78.3
Children lead	80.7	50.2	28.4	26.8	17.9
Children enjoy	96.3	82	67.8	68	87.4
Children are active	96.7	70.4	67.5	70.2	10.5
Children use a range of vocabulary	50.6	62.9	73	69.1	6.3
Children make choices	74.3	54.9	34.7	55.8	13.7
Children use a range of skills	89.1	76.4	76.9	72.6	15.8
Children make meaning through the experiences they acquire during the activity	63.2	67.9	68.4	66.9	23.2
Children attempt problem solving	66.1	67.4	70.3	56.8	55.8
Children are attentive	72.6	69.6	70.3	65.4	50.5
Children engage physically	93.2	72.6	69.1	80	4.2
Children engage emotionally	87.6	76.5	65.9	73.4	38.9

Table 2. Teachers' perspectives (%) on play-based pedagogy and digital devices (n = 920).

Statements	Strongly agree	Agree	Not sure	Disagree	Strongly disagree
Play-based pedagogy is offering an environment where children have opportunities to explore first hand experiences, enjoying and at the same time hep them to develop and learn through play	10.3	66.8	14.9	6.7	2
Play-based pedagogy is based on play where children are actively involved, self-motivated and activate their psychical, cognitive, emotional and social skills	16.7	69.1	11	2.2	1
Play-based pedagogy is based on teachers facilitating children's play for their development and learning	21.1	55.8	18.9	1.1	3.2
Play-based pedagogy is the creation of an environment where children have opportunities to re-enact life experiences for educational purposes	31.6	57.9	6.3	3.2	1.1
Play-based pedagogy is a planned educational environment where play is a central element to support children development and learning	18.7	57.8	14.3	5.6	3.6
Play-based pedagogy is an environment where children re-enact life scenarios through play	17.9	56.8	17.9	5.3	2.1
Digital devices can enhance a play-based pedagogy	33.7	46.3	18.6	1.3	0.1
Digital devices facilitate play-based pedagogy as a cooperative tool	9.5	14.7	53.7	14.7	7.4
Play-based pedagogy should include digital devices for technological continuation between home and school in order to enhance children's experiences	10.5	22.1	50.5	8.7	8.2
I integrate digital devices as part of play-based pedagogy	3.2	4.2	25.3	35.8	31.6
I integrate digital devices for educational purposes	7.4	9.4	11.6	38.9	33.7
I intend to include digital devices as part of play-based pedagogy	13.7	26.3	46.3	13.7	1.1
I intend to include digital devices for educational purposes only	11.6	33.7	38.7	8.4	7.4

Stage 2 focus groups

All participants in the survey were asked if they would participate in focus group interviews. There were two groups in each country with five teachers in each, all of whom were randomly chosen and gave their permission. Audio recording was used during the focus groups except in Kuwait where the teachers did not want to be recorded, so notes were kept during the interview. Interviews were conducted in the language of the participants.

All the interview transcripts were translated into English, before the thematic analysis took place. There was a lot of discussion about translation issues. A literal translation was initially chosen, but the data appeared unnatural and unrealistic and the naturalistic language responses of the teachers were lost. Instead, free translation was adopted in which the thematic interpretation of the interviews offered the opportunity to seek for explanations and themes that moved beyond language barriers and developed an empathy towards the data. In the presentation of the qualitative results, the chosen extracts are indicative of the points made in the thematic analysis.

Qualitative results

There was a cross-situational consistency in the thematic analysis of the focus groups interviews from which seven themes emerged:

(1) Child active vs. passive;

(2) Child as independent vs. dependent learner;
(3) Child's safety vs. risk/danger;
(4) Child as natural explorer vs. non inquisitiveness;
(5) Child as social learner vs. isolate;
(6) Child initiated play vs. directed play;
(7) Child's self-directive dispositions to learning vs. mediating, mechanical learning.

Child active vs. passive

Teachers expressed concerns about whether the digital devices encourage active or passive learning. Both of these terms were used by teachers in ambiguous ways. The typical view was that children have to be active in the classroom and thus need to move around, interact with materials, construct their understanding and experience materials 'first hand' with their senses. Conversely, teachers felt that digital devices were a secondary activity where *children see the world through a screen most of the time rather than seeing the real materials [...] how is it possible for children to understand the world through the screen of these devices? (Greek teacher)*

In regard to interactive digital toys, teachers felt that children might rely too much on what they can do rather than what can be done with them. They also felt that there is not much opportunity for active engagement in the absence of 'real materials' as the following contribution illustrates:

> but I do not get it, how a child can see the difference between let's say a rainy day and a sunny day through a digital toy? The children need to be able to see, smell the rain and then on a sunny day see the sun, smell the earth, feel [...] play is about using all the senses and physical interactions that I am not convinced digital devices offer to our children. (English teacher)

Child as independent vs. dependent learner

Teachers perceived themselves as facilitators, supporters and coaches of children's play and learning in their practice. With the digital technologies, however, they felt that: *children play on their own with these [...] there is no room for any interactions* (Maltese teacher), unlike other activities where teachers felt they could support children, such as writing, drawing or linguistic activities such as storytelling, singing and arts where the teachers *can use words, symbols, images, pictures, language* (English teacher) to share meanings. They felt that digital devices do not offer these possibilities as they are one-way interactions with children; the question was: *how can children be developed into independent learners where they are in control?* (Kuwaiti teacher).

This dichotomy between children as independent vs. dependent learners raises the argument about the role of the teacher in a play-based pedagogy. The teachers considered that digital devices limit children's independent actions, and asked how children could perform a task without assistance in the future if they are dependent on a digital device to execute the activity:

> How can children perform the activity independently? For example when we are about to play music chairs, we do explain to children how it is played, we do try and then we allow children to perform this on their own [...] I cannot see this happening with a digital toy. Or maybe I do not know how. (Luxemburg teacher)

> Play is and should be self-directed, but it seems to me that with all these technologies, children are limited to creating self-directed, self-regulated activities. The technology does it for them and they mechanically just follow the instructions, they do not have any power or control to change rules as they do with their other play. (Greek teacher)

Child safety vs. risk/danger

The discussion on this topic was around Internet-based digital devices and well-being. Teachers considered the children were too young to be exploring the Internet even with guidance. Concerns were also raised about children's physical posture when interacting with digital devices and the limited opportunities for motor development which teachers considered essential in early childhood.

Child as natural explorer vs. non inquisitiveness

Teachers agreed that children should construct their understanding of the world around them through actively exploring the environment. They used the term 'natural' environment to describe children's engagement with materials (such as leaves, fruits, pieces of wood, sea shells and animals) in the outdoor environment, including the school playground. They believed that children's engagement in play through interactions with natural materials could lead to deep learning. Conversely, digital devices could not help children to engage in the same ways as natural materials. Teachers thus did not acknowledge digital devices as providing opportunities that facilitate and support children's play.

Child as social learner vs. isolate

There were fears raised about children not interacting with other children when playing with digital devices, especially screen-based ones. Teachers considered that this could result in isolation, with the integration of digital devices hindering the social interactions of children.

Child initiated play vs. directed play

Teachers expressed concerns about the extent to which children's use of digital devices could be considered as play or free play as it is directed more by the applications or software. They considered that digital devices direct play and this indicates what teachers considered as play as opposed to what children might consider as play. The remaining question is whether play is a medium of learning and as such should lead to children's learning or is play a way for exploring and making meaning of the world around them? Digital devices might have a place as a toy.

Among focus groups, the dominant view was that play should be about children being able to learn in an enjoyable way, and that the role of the teacher is to facilitate children's play. When digital devices are used, however, it appeared that teachers felt they did not have control of these interactions and consequently of children's learning. In terms of how they see digital devices as a medium for play, they felt confused and considered that the opportunities offered by digital devices were ones which teachers could already create in the classroom.

> It is difficult, as it is, to know what is going on in their minds [children] let alone understand their perspectives. Children play and take things on board that obviously are different from ours [meaning goals of outcomes] [...] because I think we do not know really what they learn and what they get out of this, so if this is difficult how do we control all these technologies in the class?. (Maltese teacher)

Child's self-directive dispositions to learning vs. mediating, mechanical learning

Teachers were anxious that digital devices did not allow children to initiate activities, and so impeded their imagination and creativity. They felt that digital devices might lead to the acquisition of a limited range of skills. The concerns were around how children could be stimulated and how they could be offered the necessary physical contact with materials. Teachers voiced concerns that most of these toys just offer directions for use, with no space for children's imagination, and no richness in language:

> Take Minecraft, for example. [...] It is supposed to be something that children can build, construct, explore with geometrical shapes, but it is so limited to what children can do [...] when a child draws on a piece of paper they can draw a line which is not straight and they can also create shapes and designs so they are not restricted by the graphics of a game. (Luxemburg teacher)

Child inclusion or exclusion

Concerns were raised that the integration of digital devices might widen the gap between children from technologically rich homes and children from disadvantaged backgrounds who, for economic reasons, do not have the same experience to inform their use of the digital devices in the classroom. They also felt that they were not equipped, by training or guidelines, to support children who do not have experiences with digital devices at home.

> If I have them [digital devices] do I give them to the children that I know are disadvantaged and do not have opportunities at home, or do I allow equal time with children who will have them the moment they go back to their homes? This is an ethical dilemma. (Greek teacher)

It was evident during the interviews that teachers expressed concerns about children's behaviours and how they might react if their classrooms had integrated digital technologies, but that they admitted that their fears were exaggerated:

> In real life children are using them [digital devices] all the time. Last week there was a parents' evening and parents came with their children. When talking to us they gave them their smart phones for children to play and keep them busy. The children were happily contained on their own with them. (English teacher)

Discussion and conclusions

It is evident from the data that ECE teachers have fully integrated digital devices into their everyday personal lives, have positive attitudes towards them, have developed appropriate skills and were coping with their use. When it comes to their beliefs about their use in ECE, however, this study demonstrates their hesitation in integrating digital devices. This hesitation begins with their view of play-based pedagogy as a situation where children enjoy active first-hand experiences in the physical environment. Digital devices are not seen as offering such opportunities and are viewed as static and controlling children's creativity, motivation and exploration. Although the teachers did not suggest that digital devices have no role in ECE, they could not see, or were not convinced, that they could support children. They felt unprepared, unsure, confused and concerned about different recommendations for children's use of digital devices.

From the quantitative and qualitative data, it is evident that digital devices were viewed as being socially and physically limiting, directive and not offering mediated activities. Furthermore, teachers considered their use to be in opposition to what they actually try to do, believing that digital devices do not create opportunities for play in which children explore all their senses, but tend to limit both language interaction and opportunities for self-directed actions. They feared that digital devices could not support them in their role as teachers, feeling that they had very little control over how the applications were developed or how they felt as users:

> In other activities as teachers we plan, design, choose materials, but with the digital toys everything is designed for us and we just give them to children, so where does this leave us? (Maltese teacher)

These findings correspond to the work of Plowman and McPake (2013) who described seven myths that dominate the discourse of the use of digital devices at home:

- the extent to which digital devices are part of children's lives or still in the periphery of their lives;
- issues around children being isolated while interacting with devices;
- the degree of dominance in their lives;
- the tensions between play and learning;
- the extent to which technology offers opportunities to combine play and learning;
- the educational purpose of these devices considering the nature of interactions they provide;
- the problematisation of whether children need to learn to use these devices as lifelong learning skills.

This study found that similar myths still dominate teachers' attitudes towards digital devices. It seems that there is a cross-cultural consensus about the nature of play-based pedagogy, and that digital devices are not seen as offering interactions or experiences that can be considered as playful and thus part of a play-based pedagogy.

Drawing upon the theoretical underpinnings of this study, which aimed to understand how attitudes and aptitudes related to teachers' behaviours, feelings and intentions, three key dispositions can be identified – functional, emotional and cognitive – that might hinder the integration of digital devices in ECE.

Firstly, the functional dispositions are related to the voices for and against the integration of digital devices in ECE. As voices against digital devices promote scepticism on whether they should be used by children (i.e. Kabali et al. 2015; Radesky et al. 2015), teachers' readiness to create playful opportunities for their integration into ECE is shaped by concerns about children's well-being, safety and health and the risk of social isolation. Digital devices are seen as static, controlling children's creativity, socially and linguistically limiting children and not providing opportunities for mediating activities. Consequently, these functional depositions impeded the integration of digital devices.

Secondly, the emotional dispositions towards the integration of digital devices in ECE determine the impact and acceptance of digital devices in play-based pedagogy. These dispositions can be described as:

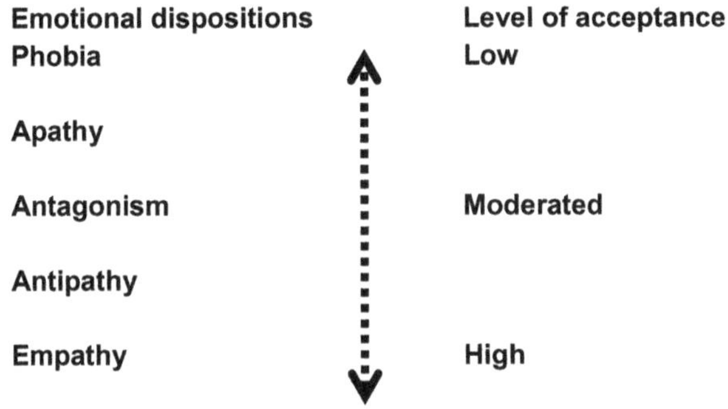

Figure 1. Emotional depositions towards digital devices in ECE.

Table 3. ECE teachers' attitudes and aptitudes towards digital devices.

Cognitive Dispositions	Characteristics	Outcome
Digitally reactive	Teachers differ their responses towards digital devices depending on the ideology they are working with because they interpret this ideology in different ways	Rejection
Digitally diffident	Teachers differ their responses towards digital devices depending on the effects they think they might have on children's behaviour	Scepticism
Digitally open	Teachers recognise children's digital experiences and the need for technological continuity between home and school	Cooperation
Digital proactive	Teachers determine their responses towards digital devices with active choices and recognise them as a cooperative tool	Integration

- *Phobia:* anxieties around the role of teacher in the integration of digital devices, and about the mediation of children's play and learning.
- *Apathy: a*voidance of discussion, or of holding an opinion, on the integration of digital devices.
- *Antagonism:* belief that children's interactions with digital devices, like the devices themselves, are controlled by manufacturers
- *Antipathy:* belief that digital devices impede social interactions and limit opportunities for creative thinking.
- *Empathy:* teachers showed responsiveness and compliance towards digital devices in ECE.

Figure 1 shows the levels of acceptance in terms of involvement.

Thirdly it is suggested that ECE teachers' attitudes reveal four cognitive dispositions towards digital devices as shown in the first column in Table 3.

Final thought

Assumptions about the nature of play-based pedagogy and the potential uses of digital devices have created tensions and confusion among teachers in ECE and have influenced their dispositions towards the integration of digital devices. Although teachers view the integration of digital devices as a potentially positive development of their practice, the dominant ideology is that play-based pedagogy leaves no space for digital devices to be included. Consequently their attitudes and aptitudes towards the use of digital devices have produced dispositions where teachers at a functional, emotional and cognitive level have been oriented by tensions as to what extent they should respond favourably or unfavourably to the integration of digital devices in their practice. This has implications for research as there is a need to review and challenge the ideology of play-based pedagogy. Similarly, it has implications for pre- and in-service training of ECE teachers. Dispositions which cause teachers to see use of digital devices as static and controlling will not promote integration and acceptance. Instead, more research is needed on how and why children are using digital devices and the nature of these interactions.

Disclosure statement

No potential conflict of interest was reported by the author.

References

Aldhafeeri, F. M., I. Palaiologou, and A. Folorunsho. 2016. "Integration of Digital Technologies in Play-based Pedagogy in Kuwaiti Early Childhood Education: Teachers' Views, Attitudes and Attributes" *International Journal of Early Years Education* 8 (1): 3–18. doi:http://dx.doi.org/10.1080/09669760.2016.1172477

Aldhafeeri, F M., and Palaiologou, I. 2016. "Interactions with Digital Technologies of Children from 3 to 6 in Kuwaiti Homes." *Educational Futures*.

Alliance for Childhood. 2004. *Tech Tonic: Towards Literacy of Technology*. College Park, MD: Alliance for Childhood.

Aubrey, C., and S. Dahl. 2014. "The Confidence and Competence in Information and Communication Technologies of Practitioners, Parents and Young Children in the Early Years Foundation Stage." *Early Years* 34 (1): 94–108.

Barrett, P. T., and P. Kline. 1982. *Factor Extraction: An Examination of Three Methods*. Person. Group Behuc.

Beetham, H., and R. Sharpe. 2007. "An Introduction to Rethink Pedagogy for a Digital Age." In *Rethinking Pedagogy for a Digital Age: Designing and Delivering E-learning*, edited by H. Beetham and R. Sharpe, 1–10. Abindgton: Routledge.

BERA ECE SIG. 2003. *Early Years Research: Pedagogy, Curriculum and Adult Roles, Training and Professionalism*. Accessed November 11, 2015. file:///C:/Users/Ioanna/AppData/Local/Microsoft/Windows/INetCache/IE/6GETA52E/beraearlyyearsreview31may03.pdf

Bergen, D. 2012. "Play, Technology Toy Affordances and Brain Development: Research Needs and Policy Issues." In *Play: A Polyphony of Research, Theories, and Issues*, edited by L. Cohen and S. Waite-Stupiansky, 164–173. Maryland: University Press of America.

Bem, D. J. 1972. "Self Perception Theory." In *Advances in Experimental Social Psychology*, edited by L. Berkowitz, Vol 6, 2–67. New York, NY: Academic Press.

Bittman, M., L. Rutherford, B. Brown, and L. Unsworth. 2011. "Digital Natives? New and Old Media and Children's Outcomes." *Australian Journal of Education* 55 (2): 161–175.

Cattell, R. B. 1973. *Personality and Mood by Questionnaire*. London: Jossey-Bass.

Chaurdon, S. 2015. *Young Children (0–8) and Digital Technologies: A Qualitative Study across Seven Countries*. Italy: Publications Office of the European Union.

Cordes, C., and E. Miller. 2000. *Fool's Gold: A Critical Look at Computers in Childhood*. Alliance for Childhood. http://www.allianceforchildhood.net/projects/computers/computers_reports.htm.

Dahlberg, G., and M. Bloch. 2006. "Is the Power to See and Visualise Always the Power to Control?" In *The Future is Not What It Appears to Be: Pedagogy, Genealogy and Political Epistemology*, edited by T. S. Popkewitz, K. Petterson, U. Ollson, and J. Kowalczyk, 39–50. Stockholm: HLS Forlag.

Edwards, S. 2013. "Digital Play in the Early Years: A Contextual Response to the Problem of Integrating Technologies and Play-Based Pedagogies in the Early Childhood Curriculum." *European Early Childhood Education Research Journal* 21 (2): 199–212.

European Early Childhood Education Research Association. 2014. *Ethical Code, the European Early Childhood Education Research Association Ethical Code (EECERA)*. Accessed April 29, 2015. www.eecera.org/ethical-code

Falloon, G. 2013. "Young Students Using IPads: App Design and Content Influences on Their Learning Pathways." *Computers and Education* 68: 505–521.

Fleer, M. 2011. "Technologically Constructed Childhoods: Moving beyond a Reproductive and Critical View of Curriculum Development." *Australasian Journal of Early Childhood* 36 (1): 16–24.

Fleer, M. 2013a. "Digital Positioning for Inclusive Practice in Early Childhood: The Cultural Practices Surrounding Digital Tablets in Family Homes." *Computers in New Zealand Schools: Learning, Teaching, Technology* 25 (1–3): 56–76.

Fleer, M. 2013b. *Theorising Play in the Early Years*. New York, NY: Cambridge University Press.

Gonzalez, M. R., and C. L. Fryer. 2012. "From Our Classroom to Their Classroom: A Community Partnership Toward Quality Early Intervention Programming." *Pennsylvania Teacher Educator* 11: 1–10.

Hatzigianni, M., and K. Margetts. 2012. "'I Am Very Good at Computers': Young Children's Computer Use and Their Computer Self-Esteem." *European Early Childhood Education Research Journal* 20: 3–20.

Hedges, H., and J. Cullen. 2011. "Participatory Learning Theories: A Framework for Early Childhood Pedagogy." *Early Child Development and Care* 82 (7): 921–940.

Hermans, R., J. Tondeur, J. van Braak, and M. Valcke. 2008. "The Impact of Primary School Teachers' Educational Beliefs on the Classroom Use of Computers." *Computers and Education* 51: 1499–1509.

Holloway, D., L. Green, and S. Livingstone. 2013. *Zero to Eight: Young Children and Their Internet Use*. LSE, London: EU Kids Online. Accessed August 1, 2015. http://eprints.lse.ac.uk/52630/

Howard, J., G. Miles, and L. Rees-Davies. 2012. "Computer Use within a Play-Based Early Years Curriculum." *International Journal of Early Years Education* 20 (2): 175–189.

Inan, F. A., and D. L. Lowther. 2010. "Factors Affecting Technology Integration in K-12 Classrooms: A Path Model." *Educational Technology Research and Development* 58: 137–154.

Jowett, E. L., D. W. Moore, and A. Anderson. 2012. "Using an iPad-based Video Modelling Package to Teach Numeracy Skills to a Child with an Autism Spectrum Disorder." *Developmental Neurorehabilitation* 15 (4): 304–312. doi:http://dx.doi.org/10.3109/17518423.2012.682168.

Kabali, H. K., M. Matilde Irigoyen, R. Nunez-Davis, J. G. Budacki, S. H. Mohanty, K. P. Leister, and R. L. Bonner Jr. 2015. "Exposure and Use of Mobile Media Devices by Young Children." *Pediatrics* 136 (6): 1044–1050.

Kalas, I. 2010. *Recognizing the Potential of ICT in Early Childhood Education*. Moscow: UNESCO Institute for Information Technologies in Education.

Katz, D. 1960. "The Functional Approach to the Study of Attitudes." *Public Opinion Quarterly* 24: 163–204.

Kerckaert, S., S. R. Ruben Vanderlinde, and J. van Braak. 2015. "The Role of ICT in Early Childhood Education: Scale Development and Research on ICT Use and Influencing Factors." *European Early Childhood Education Research Journal* 23 (2): 183–199. doi:http://dx.doi.org/10.1080/1350293X.2015.1016804.

Kirkorian, H. L., T. A. Pempek, L. A. Murphy, M. E. Schmidt, and D. R. Anderson. 2009. "The Impact of Background Television on Parent-Child Interaction." *Child Development*. 80 (5): 1350–1359.

Levin, T., and R. Wadmany. 2008. "Teachers' Views on Factors Affecting Effective Integration of Information Technology in the Classroom: Developmental Scenery." *Jl of Technology and Techer Education* 16 (2): 233–263.

Lindahl, M.-G., and A.-M. Folkesson. 2012a. "ICT in Preschool: Friend or Foe? The Significance of Norms in a Changing Practice." *International Journal of Early Years Education* 20 (4): 422–436.

Lindahl, M.-G., and A.-M. Folkesson. 2012b. "Can We Let Computers Change Practice? Educators' Interpretations of Preschool Tradition." *Computers in Human Behavior* 28 (5): 1728–1737.

Livingstone, S., G. Mascheroni, M. Dreier, S. Chaudron, and K. Lagae. 2015. *How Parents of Young Children Manage Digital Devices at Home: The Role of Income, Education and Parental Style*. London: EU Kids Online, LSE.

Marsh, J. 2010. "Young Children's Play in Online Virtual Worlds." *Journal of Early Childhood Research* 8: 23–39.

Marsh, J. 2012. "Purposes for Literacy in Children's use of the Online Virtual World 'Club Penguin'." *Journal of Research in Reading*. doi:http://dx.doi.org/10.1111/j.1467-9817.2012.01530.x.

Marsh, J., and J. C. Bishop. 2014. *Changing Play: Play, Media and the Commercial Culture from 1950s to the Present Day*. Maidenhead: Open University Press.

Marsh, J., G. Brooks, J. Hughes, L. Ritchie, S. Roberts, and K. Wright. 2005. *Digital Beginnings: Young Children's Use of Popular Culture, Media*. University of Sheffield: Literacy Research Centre.

Melhuish, K., and G. Falloon. 2010. "Looking to the Future: M-Learning with the iPad." *Computers in New Zealand Schools: Learning, Leading, Technology* 22 (30): 1–15.

Mills, S. C., and R. C. Tincher. 2003. "Be the Technology." *Journal of Research on Technology in Education* 35 (3): 382–401.

Morgan, A. 2010. "Interactive Whiteboards, Interactivity and Play in the Classroom with Children Aged Three to Seven Years." *European Early Childhood Education Research Journal* 18: 93–104.

Moyles, J., S. Adams, and A. Musgrove. 2002. *SPEEL Study of Pedagogical Effectiveness. Research Report 363*. London: Department for Education and Skills.

Nash, L. 2012. "Exploring iPads in Learning." *Learning and Teaching* 31: 7–13.

Nikolopoulou, K., and V. Gialamas. 2015a. "ICT and Play in Preschool: Early Childhood Teachers' Beliefs and Confidence." *International Journal of Early Years Education* 23 (4): 409–425. doi:http://dx.doi.org/10.1080/09669760.2015.1078727.

Nikolopoulou, K., and V. Gialamas. 2015b. "Barriers to the Integration of Computers in Early Childhood Settings: Teachers' Perceptions." *Education and Information Technologies* 20 (2): 285–301.

Ólafsson, K., Livingstone, S., and Haddon, L. 2014. *Children's Use of Online Technologies in Europe: A Review of the European Evidence Base*. LSE, London: EU Kids Online. Second edition. Accessed November 25, 2015. www.lse.ac.uk/media@lse/research/EUKidsOnline/EU%20Kids%20III/Reports/D2.2RevisedEvidenceReview_sept2014.pdf33

Palaiologou, I. 2014. "Children under Five and Digital Technologies: Implication for Early Years Pedagogy." *The European Early Childhood Research Journal* 24 (1) (printed copy publication 2016). doi:http://dx.doi.org/10.1080/1350293X.2014.929876.

Palaiologou, I. 2016. "Children Under Five and Digital Technologies: Implication for Early Years Pedagogy." *The European Early Childhood Research Journal* 24 (1): 5–24. doi:http://dx.doi.org/10.1080/1350293X.2014.929876

Palmer, S. 2006. *Toxic Childhood: How the Modern World is Damaging Our Children and What We Can Do about It*. London: Orion Books.

Palmer, S. 2008. *Detoxing Childhood: What Parents Need to Know to Raise Happy, Successful Children: What Parents Need to Know to Raise Bright, Balanced Children*. London: Orion Books.

Parette, H., and C. Blum. 2013. *Instructional Technology in Early Childhood: Teaching in the Digital Age*. Baltimore, MD: Brookes.

Plowman, L. 2015. "Researching Young Children's Everyday uses of Technology in the Family Home." *Open access in Interacting with Computers* 27 (1): 36–46.

Plowman, L., and J. McPake. 2013. "Seven Myths about Young Children and Technology." *Childhood Education* 89 (1): 27–33.

Plowman, L., and C. Stephen. 2005. "Children, Play, and Computers in Pre-School Education." *British Journal of Educational Technology* 36: 145–157.

Plowman, L., J. McPake, and C. Stephen. 2008. "Just Picking It up? Young Children Learning with Technology at Home." *Cambridge Journal of Education* 38 (3): 303–319.

Radesky J. S., C. J. Kistin, B. Zuckerman, K. Nitzberg, J. Gross, M. Kaplan-Sanoff, M. Augustyn, and M. Silverstein. 2014. "Patterns of Mobile Device Use by Caregivers and Children during Meals in Fast Food Restaurants." *Pediatrics* 133 (4). www.pediatrics.org/cgi/content/full/133/4/e843

Radesky J. S., C. Kistin, S. Eisenberg, B. Zuckerman, and M. Silverstein. 2015. *Parent Views about Mobile Device use around and by Young Children: Implications for Anticipatory Guidance*. Abstract presented at the Pediatric Academic Societies, San Diego, CA. Accessed Feb 4, 2016. www.abstracts2view.com/pas/view.php?nu=PAS15L1_2195.2

Rideout, V., U. G. Foehr, and D. Roberts. 2010. *Generation M2: Media in the Lives of 8- to 18-Year-Olds*. Menlo Park, CA: Henry J. Kaiser Family Foundation.

Roseberry, S., K. Hirsh-Pasek, and R. M. Golinkoff. 2014. "Skype Me! Socially Contingent Interactions Help Toddlers Learn Language." *Child Development* 85 (3): 956–970.

Sang, G., M. Valcke, J. van Braak, and J. Tondeur. 2010. "Student Teachers' Thinking Processes and ICT Integration: Predictors of Prospective Teaching Behaviors with Educational Technology." *Computers & Education* 54: 103–112.

Schachter, S. 1964. "The Interaction of Cognitive and Psychological Determinants of Emotional State." In *Advances in Experimental Social Psychology*, edited by L. Berkowitz, Vol 1, 49–80. New York, NY: Academic Press.

Sewlyn, N. 2011. *Schools and Schooling in Digital Age*. Abington: Routledge.

Smerdon, B., S. Cronen, L. Lanahan, J. Anderson, N. Iannotti, and J. Angeles. 2000. *Teachers' Tools for the 21st Century: A Report on Teachers' Use of Technology (NCES 2000–102)*. Washington, DC: U.S. Department of Education, National Center for Education Statistics.

Stahlberg, D. and D. Frey. 1988. "Attitudes, 1: Structure, Measurement and Functions." In *Introduction to Social Psychology*, edited by H. Hewstone, W. Stroebe, J. B. Codol and G. M. Stephenson, 132–187. Oxford: Blackwell.

Stephen, C. 2010. "Pedagogy: The Silent Partner in Early Years Learning." *Early Years* 30 (1): 15–28.

Taguchi, L. H. 2010. *Going Beyond the Theory/Practice Divide in Early Childhood Education*. Abingdon: Routledge.

Terreni, L. 2011. "Interactive Whiteboards, Art and Young Children." *Computers in New Zealand Schools: Learning, Teaching, Technology* 23 (1): 78–100.

Teuwens, J. 2011. "Het gebruik van internet door preschoolers." [The Use of the Internet by Preschoolers.] Unpublished Master's dissertation. Brussels: Department of Educational Studies, Ghent University.

Verenikina, I., and L. Kervin. 2011. "IPads, Digital Play and Pre-schoolers." *He Kupu* 2 (5): 4–19.

Wartella, E. 2013. *Parenting in the Age of Digital Technology: A National Survey, Canter on Media and Human Development, School of Communication*. California: Northwester University.

Weiner, B. 1986. *An Attributional Theory of Motivation and Emotion*. New York: Springer-Verlag.

Wood, E. 2014. "Reconceptualising the Play-pedagogy Relationship." In *Sage Handbook of Play and Learning in Early Childhood*, edited by L. Brooker, M. Blaise, and S. Edwards, 145–156. London: Sage.

Wood, E., J. Specht, T. Willoughby, and J. Mueller. 2008. "Integrating Computer Technology in Early Childhood Education Environments: Issues Raised by Early Childhood Educators." *The Alberia Journal of Educational Research* 54: 210–226.

Yelland, N. J. 2011. "Knowledge Building with ICT in the Early Years of Schooling." *He Kupu*. 2 (5): 33–44.

Developing a measure to understand young children's Internet cognition and cyber-safety awareness: a pilot test

Susan Edwards, Andrea Nolan, Michael Henderson, Helen Skouteris,
Ana Mantilla, Pamela Lambert and Jo Bird

ABSTRACT

Advancements in technology have increased preschool children's access to the Internet. Very little research has been conducted to identify pre-school-aged children's understandings of the Internet and ramifications of being 'online'. Without an understanding of children's thinking about the Internet, it is difficult to provide age- and pedagogically appropriate cyber-safety education. This study developed and pilot-tested an interview schedule that focuses on the Internet thinking and cyber-safety awareness of Australian children aged 4–5 years. The schedule is informed by sociocultural theory, cyber-safety education research and approaches for researching with young children. The schedule shows potential to elicit children's understandings of the Internet and cyber-safety awareness. Adjustments are required to allow more contextualised responses from children.

Introduction

For the first time in the history of early childhood education, the field is faced with the problem of how to best provide young children with age-relevant and pedagogically appropriate cyber-safety education. This problem exists because touch screen mobile technologies have quite literally put the Internet at the fingertips of preschoolers. International research indicates rapid uptake of these technologies and young children's consequent Internet access in the years since the release of the first iPhone in 2007 (Holloway, Green, and Livingstone 2013; Livingstone, Haddon, and Görzig 2012). Known as 'digitods' (Gold 2015), this generation of children has never experienced a time when the Internet could not be accessed via the swipe of a finger on a mobile device – anywhere, any time. Coupled with a digital footprint created by parents, caregivers or relatives (often even before they are born), digitods are online via social media, the use of Internet-enabled apps, the consumption of digital media using on-demand streaming or social networking sites, and by participation in child-centred websites (O'Keeffe and Clarke-Pearson 2011). With digitods online in increasing numbers, the development of cyber-safety education appropriate for the learning needs of the very young is becoming pressing. However, research into the cyber-safety education of young children is not only limited, but understandings of the precursor concept to cyber-safety education in terms of *what pre-school-aged children understand the Internet to be* are almost non-existent.

We have begun to address this problem through the concept of 'Internet cognition' (Edwards et al. 2015). Previously, we defined Internet cognition as young children's understandings of the Internet. We considered 'cognition' from a sociocultural perspective as children's acquisition of cultural knowledge through social interaction and the use of physical and conceptual tools (Daniels 2008; Vygotsky 1997). We defined the 'Internet' in terms of two main concepts – technical and social. A technical definition of the Internet: as an 'association of computer networks with common standards which enable messages to be sent from any central host on one network to any host on another' (Crystal 2001; 2–3); and a social definition of the Internet: as enabling positive and negative social impact for people (Yan 2005). We are now interested in better understanding young children's internet cognition so that educators can use what is known about children's thinking of the Internet as a platform for preschool-aged children's cyber-safety education. Children's understanding of the Internet should provide a platform for cyber-safety education because the field is historically committed to planning learning experiences based on children's existing understandings of world phenomena (Johnson 2014). Existing work tends to adapt current approaches for cyber-safety education intended for older primary and secondary school-aged children for young children, and so advocates using filters and/or adult-imposed safety rules (Grey 2011) instead of building children's agency for keeping themselves safe online. There are also pedagogical issues in adapting existing approaches, such as providing young children with colouring-in sheets in the hope that this will increase their levels of cyber-safety awareness (e.g. Australian Government & Australian Communications and Media Authority 2015). We suggest children's understanding of the Internet should inform their cyber-safety education because these conceptions are likely to influence how and why children are able to identify the need for cyber-safety practices in the first instance.

Given the lack of research knowledge into: (a) what young children think the Internet is; and (b) their likely responses to a range of cyber-safety scenarios; we set out to develop an interview schedule to gain insight into these issues. Our intention was that the responses from children would be used by educators to inform the development of cyber-safety learning experiences for enactment in the children's classrooms. To this end, we acknowledge that the work of this paper is largely exploratory – opening a new area of investigation in the absence of existing research about the Internet cognition and cyber-safety awareness of preschool-aged children.

In this paper, we therefore discuss the theoretical and empirical literature informing the initial development of the schedule. When we set out to develop the schedule, we found little previous research to guide the range of questions we thought suitable for asking preschool-aged children about their understandings of the Internet and cyber-safety awareness. We therefore defined the questions in the first version of the schedule according to considerations derived from three bodies of empirical and policy-based literature including: (1) sociocultural theory as a theoretical perspective used for researching young children's technology use (Plowman, McPake, and Stephen 2010); (2) research literature into children's understanding of the internet and cyber-safety awareness (Ey and Cupit 2011; Yan 2009);

and (3) appropriate research methods for working with young children (Groundwater-Smith, Dockett, and Bottrell 2015).

We commence the paper with an overview of the considerations from these three bodies of literature. We then describe the development and process of piloting the schedule with 71 4- to 5-year-old Australian children. Finally, we reflect on our learning from the development and pilot trial of the schedule. We also consider implications for future development of the schedule as a tool for helping educators develop age-relevant and pedagogically appropriate cyber-safety education for young children.

Overview of the considerations from the main bodies of empirical and policy-based literature

Sociocultural perspectives on young children's technology use and learning

Sociocultural theory is a well-accepted theoretical perspective used in research about young children's technology use. The complexity of children's technology use both in the home and in educational and community settings from a sociocultural perspective includes: how children interact with parents and caregivers during technology use (Livingstone et al. 2015; Plowman, McPake, and Stephen 2008); the role of peer to peer engagement in fostering technological skills/knowledge/attitudes (Plowman and McPake 2013); and social practices associated with technology use in children's daily lives (Fleer 2013). Research reporting on children's technology use at home, and in educational settings, frequently draws on socio-culturally informed literature including ideas derived from the work of Vygotsky (Verenikina and Kervin 2011), social constructionism, the co-creation of funds of knowledge and communities of practice (Holloway, Green, and Stevenson 2015).

We likewise used sociocultural ideas to inform the development of our schedule. This perspective positions children's cognition as built-through relationships with social peers and adults using both the physical and conceptual tools of their host community (Stetsenko 2011). The concept of tool mediation is central to this process and explains how people come to use and master tools to achieve the object of their activity (Vygotsky 1997). For young children, tool mediation is supported by interactions with peers, older children and/or adults in how to use a tool, or through observing others using a tool. Tools can be either conceptual or physical. We were interested in the technologies as tools and the social practices associated with the object of activity in using the tool for online engagement, such as using an app, visiting a website, watching video and/or online communication (e.g. Skype). Initially, we understood technology as tool as referring to children's identification of the technologies and apps most likely to involve Internet engagement. Mastery of a tool always presupposes a changed object of activity (Vygotsky 1997). In terms of children's thinking about the Internet, this would mean understanding how a technology enables online activity over any other given tool.

Research into children's understandings of the internet and cyber-safety awareness

Very little research has been conducted into children's understandings of the Internet. The main body of work in this area is by Greenfield and Yan (2006) and Yan (2005, 2009). Yan's (2005, 2009) work divides the 'Internet' into two main aspects. The first aspect pertains to

Table 1. Children's understanding of the internet according to technical and social aspects (from Yan, 2010, 107–108).

Category	Technical	Social
Minimal	Perception-based knowledge about the internet, e.g. thinking one computer or technology represents the internet	Perception-based knowledge about social use of the internet indicating very little awareness of the positive or negative social consequence of the internet e.g. thinking the internet would never hurt a person
Partial	Perception-bounded knowledge about the internet, e.g. thinking one or several connected computers or technologies represent the internet	Perception-bounded knowledge about the social use of the internet indicating a general but limited sense of the positive or negative social consequences of the internet, e.g. seeing too many advertisements or sending a hurtful message
Extended	Conception-bounded understanding of the internet, e.g. thinking of computing centre linked to multiple other computers	Concept-bounded knowledge about the internet indicating a clear understanding of the profound social consequences of the internet, e.g. online privacy
Correct	Conception-based understanding of the internet, e.g. thinking of a system comprising networks of networks	Conception-based knowledge about the internet indicating balanced and comprehensive understanding of the profound positive and negative social consequences of the internet, e.g. password and identity protection, hackers, use for social good

the technical dimension of the Internet. This describes the Internet as a complex system originating from many networks, computers, users and application programmes, across the world (Yan 2005). The second aspect considers the social dimensions of the Internet. This focuses on the use and engagement of the Internet by people for positive (social networking, entertainment, education, research, social connection) and/or negative reasons (phishing, cyber-bullying and paedophilia) (Yan 2005). Yan's research established that children's understandings of the Internet fit into four main categories for each aspect (see Table 1).

We were interested in the finding that children could be perceptually bound in their thinking about the Internet, viewing it as the computer or technology they were using at the time (Yan 2009). Perceptual bounding led to conceptual limitations by children in which the Internet was not viewed as having the potential to be either helpful or harmful to people. A later study by Dodge, Husain, and Duke (2011) reached similar conclusions to Yan (2009) regarding the perceptual and conceptual bounding of children's Internet cognition, yet also argued that children's social understandings of the Internet were strongly linked with how and where they were most likely to use the internet on a daily basis. To date, little to no research has been conducted on the Internet cognition of very young children including 4- to 5-year olds, and/or the relationship between digitods' use of Internet-enabled touch screen devices and their consequent understanding of the Internet.

The development of our schedule was informed by our reading of Yan's (2005, 2009) and Dodge, Husain, and Duke's (2011) work. We considered the idea of children being perceptually and conceptually bound in their understanding of the Internet. From a tool-mediated perspective, we focused on children's knowledge of which 'tools' and later, which 'apps' children associated with the capacity to use the Internet. We were also interested in the extent to which children's understandings of the Internet, and their perspectives on cyber-safety practices, related to technology use *in context* rather than an abstraction of what constituted a correct view of the technical and social aspects of the Internet. This is because Yan's (2009) categories of Internet understanding were based on adult responses to the same questions posed to children–but with adults assumed to hold the more correct version.

According to research into children's understanding of scientific concepts, children's explanations for different phenomena are often contextually grounded and make sense to them according to what they experience in their daily lives (Fleer and Hardy 1993; Robbins 2005). This research suggests a contextually relevant response to children's Internet cognition should be considered, rather than one that is 'minimal' or 'partial' (Yan 2009). Contextually relevant responses were also likely to be more useful to educators for understanding children's Internet cognition as a platform for cyber-safety education in the early years.

Cyber-safety awareness is a topic of education that attracts attention as a critical contemporary learning need for all children (Giant 2013). The literature is diverse, and ranges from moral panic regarding children's exposure to unsavoury aspects of the Internet, to more measured responses and arguments regarding the pros and cons of children's Internet use (Saracho 2015). Predominant discourse focuses on active cyber-safety education given the range of skills children are now considered to need in terms of protecting their privacy, presenting themselves online, bullying, sexting, access to pornography, meeting new contacts online, excessive Internet use and exposure to advertising (Livingstone, Haddon, and Görzig 2012). Research into children's cyber-safety awareness is mainly conducted with primary and secondary school-aged children. It considers issues such as cyber-bullying, personal safety when online and computer security (O'Keeffe and Clarke-Pearson (2011). Targeted educational strategies and programmes (e.g. FBI-SOS n.d.; Education Bureau Hong Kong, 2013; ThinkUKnow Corporate Report [2014] 2015; United Kingdom Safer Internet Centre 2013) for these age groups are increasingly available. Cyber-safety education is also integrated into curriculum for primary- and secondary-aged children. For example: the Australian Curriculum Foundation to Year 10, Digital Technologies Processes and Production Skills (Australian Curriculum and Assessment Reporting Authority [ACARA], 2014) and the Computing Programme of Study Key Stage 1 and 2, and Key Stage 3 and 4 (Department of Education [DoE], 2014).

There is a paucity of developments that focus directly on the cyber-safety learning needs of pre-school-aged (4–5 years) children. Research by Ey and Cupit (2011) reporting risks identified by 5- to 8-year olds online is amongst the closest to identifying young children's cyber-safety learning needs. They found that children considered inappropriate content, meeting people online and pop-ups (online web advertisements designed to attract web traffic and capture contact information) as potential Internet risks. Grey (2011) considered the need for cyber-safety education provision in the years prior to school. However, rather than describing appropriate approaches to cyber-safety education for the early years, this paper adapts existing strategies intended for older children. A similar publication by Heider (2015) likewise promotes cyber-safety strategies typically advised for children in primary and/or secondary school. A study by Spink et al. (2010) into the web-searching strategies of preschoolers confirmed the online activities of young children, and indicated children's capacity for creating web-queries, browsing and making information-processing decisions. This study concluded that the web-searching strategies of preschool-aged children are qualitatively different from those of older children, thus prompting the increased need for specialised pedagogical approaches to online education in the early years.

The Australian Early Years Learning Framework advocates the use of technologies as a Learning Outcome for children under 'Children are effective communicators' (DEEWR, 2009, 44), but does not specifically engage with the notion of cyber-safety education. The Early Years Foundation Stage (DfE, 2014) also neither mentions online activity by young children nor cyber-safety education. The National Association for the Education of Young Children's position statement (NAEYC 2012) on technology use with young children considers online safety an aspect of 'Digital Citizenship' (10) – but does not describe pedagogical approaches towards cyber-safety education for preschoolers. Meanwhile, the first recommendation from the Australian 2011 Joint Select Committee on Cyber-Safety Report *High Wire Act: Cyber-safety and the Young* focused directly on the: 'feasibility of assisting preschools and kindergartens to provide cyber-safety educational programmes for children as part of their development activities' (5). Later in the report, it was indicated that a programme called '*Cyber-smart for young kids*' would benefit the provision of preschool cyber-safety education. However, this programme, now available through the Office of the Children's eSafety Commissioner (Commissioner Commonwealth of Australia 2015) targets the first three years of primary school rather than focusing specifically on the age-related and pedagogical needs of children aged 4–5 years. Similar issues appear with support offered in the UK and US, through the UK Safer Internet Centre and the FBI-SOS online programme, both of which are targeted towards the needs of older children.

In the absence of documented research regarding: (1) young children's awareness of cyber-safety issues; and (2) pedagogical approaches to cyber-safety education in the early years, we therefore drew on existing frameworks for thinking about cyber-safety education to develop our schedule. We focused on three main aspects of cyber-safety education: cyber-bullying; personal information; and computer security (Lindsay et al. 2011; Livingstone et al. 2015). We were interested in how children were likely to respond to a series of scenarios reflecting each of these aspects in a typical context (e.g. encountering a pop-up when playing a game).

Appropriate methods for researching with young children

Methods for researching with young children have undergone considerable development under the 'researching with children' movement. This body of literature consistently cites Article 12 of the United Nations Convention on the Rights of the Child (1989), including the statement that children have the right to speak of matters that concern them as an informing principle for researching with young children (Freeman 2009). Broadly, research with children is considered in terms of children's degree of participation in defining and conducting the research, to the consequent selection of appropriate methods for researching with young children. Hart's (2008) concept of the 'ladder of participation' provided a way for researchers to reflect on the extent to which children are being actively involved in research compared with being 'researched on'. Alderson (2005) describes three levels of research, with mid-level research describing situations where children are informed and invited to participate in adult-initiated research with consent, higher level research that is entirely child initiated, and lower level research involving little contribution from children. Changing perspectives regarding children's involvement in research has informed the development of appropriate methods for researching with young children. These methods are intended to better understand children's perspectives on matters that concern them (Nolan, Macfarlane, and Cartmel 2013). Methods include: inviting children to draw, responding to stimulus materials, interview questions, video/digital photography, documented tours and conversations with children (Fargas-Malet et al. 2010).

When developing the schedule, we selected methods 'fit for purpose' (Groundwater-Smith, Dockett, and Bottrell 2015; Punch 2002) for researching with children, and in relation to what we were interested in learning about their Internet cognition and cyber-safety awareness. This included: images of life-sized laminated iPads, icons and apps that we invited children to manipulate; questions about their own Internet use; completing drawings of the Internet (see for example, Yan 2005); and narratives involving two fictional pre-school-aged children, 'Harn' and 'Ella', in a series of cyber-safety scenarios.

Developing and piloting the schedule

Development

Initial development of the schedule focused on the considerations identified from the literature, including: (1) sociocultural perspectives on young children's technology use; and (2) research into children's understandings of the Internet and cyber-safety awareness. For sociocultural perspectives on children's technology use, we nominated: (a) technology as tool; (b) mastery of tool indicating how technologies enable Internet access over other tools; and (c) social practices associated with the object of activity [e.g. online engagement]. For research into children's Internet understanding and cyber-safety awareness, we nominated: (d) perceptual bounding [technical and/or social]; (e) conceptual bounding [technical and/or social]; and (f) cyber-safety practices in context.

Several questions for each of the six (a–f) nominated considerations were drafted and circulated around the research team for discussion and refinement. We then conceptualised the schedule in two parts with Part 1 focusing on Technology and Internet Recognition, and Part 2 on Cyber-safety. Five questions were assigned to Part 1 and 14 questions to Part 2.

We then considered approaches for researching with children for each question, using the notion of 'fit for purpose' (Punch 2002). Fit for purpose approaches are those thought suitable for young children's capacity to engage in research and for examining the research questions under consideration (Groundwater-Smith, Dockett, and Bottrell 2015). For Part 1, which focused on technology as tool, mastery of tool and social practices online, we used pictorial cues. These included a laminated life-sized iPad and icons in which children were invited to use familiar apps and icons and to identify those they thought would take them online. We also used a series of laminated objects (e.g. book, newspaper, magazine) and technologies (e.g. iPad, laptop, mobile phone) to identify which of these children understood as technological tools and technologies most likely to enable Internet access. For Part 2, which focused on cyber-safety education, we also used pictorial cues with examples of pop-ups or invitations from online games asking children to provide personal information. We also used a narrative with accompanying pictures of Harn and Ella engaged in a series of cyber-safety events. Children were invited to record their responses to these events using a traffic-light system. Finally, children were invited to draw a picture of the Internet (Yan 2005).

Table 2 summarises the interview schedule we piloted. This table shows alignment of the schedule questions across the two main parts according to the six (a-f) nominated considerations from the literature regarding sociocultural perspectives on children's technology use, and children's understandings of the Internet and cyber-safety awareness. Approaches used for researching with children for each question are also shown.

Table 2. Draft interview schedule for establishing children's internet cognition and cyber-safety awareness.

Questions	Six nominated considerations (a) Technology as tool	(b) Mastery of tool indicating how technologies enable internet access over other tools	(c) Social practices associated with object of activity (online engagement)	(d) Perceptual bounding (technical and/or social)	(e) Conceptual bounding (technical and/or social)	(f) Cyber-safety practices in context	Approach	
Part 1: Technology and Internet Recognition	1. Have you heard of the internet? What can you tell me about the internet? Who do you know uses the internet? [If no to the 'internet 'ask 'web' and/'online']			✓	✓	✓		Interview question
	2. I would like to show you some pictures of different things. Can you tell me what these are called?	✓						Pictorial cue
	3. Can we look at these pictures again? Which ones can you use to go the internet/web/online?		✓					Pictorial cue
	4. Here is an iPad and here are some icons. Can you show me which icons you know that belong on an iPad? Do you know the name of these icons? Can you tell me what that icon does?	✓	✓					Pictorial cue
	5. Let's look at the icons you have put on the iPad. Does this one take you to the internet/online/web? [checking each placed icon] How do you know this one takes you/does not take you to the internet?		✓		✓			Pictorial cue
Part 2: Cyber-safety	6. I am going to tell you a story about two children named Harn and Ella [show picture of each as their name is stated]. They like to play on Pocoyo World. When Harn or Ella play in Pocoyo World should they tell other people who are playing in Pocoyo World what their name is? [use traffic light: red/orange/green]					✓	✓	Response to narrative Pictorial cue
	7. When Harn and Ella play in Pocoyo World should they tell other people who are playing there where they live? [use traffic light: red/orange/green]. Why/why not?					✓	✓	Response to narrative Pictorial cue
	8. When Harn and Ella play in Pocoyo World should they tell other people who are playing there how old they are? [use traffic light: red/orange/green] Why/why not?					✓	✓	Response to narrative Pictorial cue

9. Here are Harn and Ella again. Ella took a photograph of Harn. Then she made the photograph look all wobbly using the photograph app. Ella thought the photograph was very funny. She printed the photograph and showed it to all Harn's friends. Harn's friends laughed at him. Do you think Ella should do this to Harn's photograph? [use traffic light: red/orange/green]. Why/why not?					✓	✓	Response to narrative Pictorial cue
10. Harn was cross with Ella because she made everyone laugh at his photograph. Harn used the iPad to make a video of Ella playing with her friends at kindergarten. He showed the video to his friends and say 'Ella is silly'. Do you think Harn should take a video of Ella and show it to his friends? [use traffic light: red/orange/green]. Why/why not?					✓	✓	Response to narrative Pictorial cue
11. What do you think Harn and Ella could do when someone takes a silly photograph or video of them? Why/why not?						✓	Interview question
12. Do you know what a pop-up is?	✓						Interview question
13. If you see pop-ups when you are playing a game on the iPad or phone what do you do?	✓						Interview question
14. Ella was playing a Mike the Knight game on the internet. A little box popped up on the screen [show image]. It had lots of colourful balloons and a 'press play' button in it. What do you think that button means? Do you think Ella should press the play button? Why/why not? [use traffic light: red/orange/green]				✓	✓	✓	Response to narrative Pictorial cue
15. Harn was playing a Yo Gabba Gabba game on the internet. A little box popped up on the screen. It had a picture of a little computer on it. The computer had a thermometer to show it was sick and it was crying. The box had a picture of a Band-Aid on it. Do you think Harn should click the Band-Aid. Why/why not? [use traffic light: red/orange/green]				✓	✓	✓	Response to narrative Pictorial cue
16. Do you use the iPad/phone/laptop with someone or by yourself?			✓				Interview question
17. Do you have to ask anyone if you can these?			✓				Interview question
18. Can you tell me what you do on the iPad/phone/laptop?	✓	✓					Interview question
19. Could you please draw a picture for me of what you think the internet/online/web looks like?	✓			✓	✓		Drawing

Pilot testing

The schedule was piloted in the context of a broader study we were conducting about the development of cyber-safety learning experiences by teachers. The project was conducted with ethical approval from our universities and from the State Education Department. In the broader study, we were using the schedule to generate stimulus material about the children's Internet cognition and cyber-safety awareness that their educators could draw on to inform the development of specific cyber-safety learning experiences for preschool-aged children. The broader study was conducted as a randomised trial. Two groups of educators and children participated; one group was randomised to an intervention group and the other group to a control group. Educators in the intervention group received access to the children's responses to the schedule and attended a professional learning session about cyber-safety. The control group continued practice as usual. The purpose of the randomisation was to ascertain the influence, if any, on pre-school-aged children's participation in learning experiences about cyber-safety on their Internet cognition and levels of cyber-safety awareness. The interview schedule was administered to children in both the intervention and control groups before and after intervention.

The intervention group included 48 children, and the control group 23 children. All children were aged between 4 and 5 years at the time of piloting. Children were attending a sessional 4-year-old kindergarten in a middle-to-upper socioeconomic area of Melbourne, Australia. The community rating for child development in the area was above the State and National 'on track' percentage for physical, emotional, social, language and communication development according to the Australian Early Development Census (AEDC, 2015).

Parental consent was obtained for participating children. Parents used an explanatory statement and consent form designed for child understanding to determine children's assent for project participation (Dockett, Einarsdottir, and Perry 2011). The schedule was piloted with children onsite in the main kindergarten room during a typical kindergarten session. Children's responses to the schedule were audio recorded and photographed (e.g. placement of icons on the iPad) with parental and child permission. The interview schedule took approximately 15 minutes to administer per child. Our focus in this paper is on the development of the schedule in relation to the three main bodies of empirical and policy-based literature. This means that we do not report directly on the children's responses.

Lessons learned and implications for further development of the schedule

We have not been able to identify an existing schedule that focuses on the Internet cognition and cyber-safety awareness of 4- to 5-year-old children. Developing and piloting our schedule suggested two areas for future development. First, Part 1 of the schedule did not provide sufficient opportunity for the children to explain their understandings of the Internet. This can be addressed by moving questions 16, 17, 18 and 19 from Part 2, into Part 1. However, the concept of 'technology as tool' underpinning questions regarding the artefacts likely to involve children in using the Internet (including apps) did not afford sufficient insight into children's technical and social understandings of the Internet. This is because our initial definition of technology as tool did not sufficiently encompass social practices associated with tool use. These questions were also problematic because some apps were connected to the Internet for the purposes of obtaining back data without taking children directly online (back data occur when an app mines information about end-user engagement with an app and sends this directly to the host company). This means questions about which apps were most likely to take children to the Internet (or which technologies use the Internet) do not provide sufficient insight into children's mastery of tool use with respect to online activity. Question 18, regarding children's activities on touch screen technologies provided increased opportunity for *children to discuss what they were likely to do on the Internet*, than did questions 2–5 which asked children to indicate which technologies and/or apps they associated with the Internet. Future development of Part 1 of the schedule will therefore include adjustments to the opening questions so that the schedule commences with laminated pictures of a mobile phone, iPad and/or laptop computer and invites children to select which of these are their most regularly used technologies. Children will then be invited to discuss how they use these specific technologies prior to identifying which ones take them online. Children's responses will then draw more readily on their experiences of using technologies, rather than focusing on technologies likely to access the Internet. This adjustment is significant because approaches to researching with children emphasise the role of contextual knowledge on children's responses to interview questions and/or tasks (Langston et al. 2004). Opening the schedule with a focus on children's experiences using technologies will also provide a more logical reason for inviting children to draw a picture of the Internet, and how they understand their selected technology to use the Internet. A more contextualised response from the children will also be of increased pedagogical value for educators because it will help to establish what the children know about the technologies in terms of online activity, not just tools they can identify as likely to enable Internet use over others.

Reliability testing of the schedule indicated that children's responses to questions 6–15 were stable across two time points. However, piloting also suggested that we use narrative scenarios more strongly connected with children's knowledge of technologies and apps. This could be achieved by linking the apps and technologies children indicate as known to them in Part 1, to the questions asked of them in the scenarios. For example, if a child indicates knowledge of a Peppa Pig app, this knowledge should be incorporated into the narrative scenario: e.g. 'Ella was playing a Peppa Pig game .... Some balloons popped up and a press play button ...' Instead of asking the children: 'Do you think Ella should press the play button?', the question should be rephrased as: 'If you were playing this game would *you* press the play button?' Increased opportunity for discussion beyond using the traffic-light system would also be helpful for providing educators with insight into children's justifications for their actions. This is in contrast to simply establishing if they think it is appropriate or inappropriate to click on a pop-up and/or reveal personal information in an online situation. Here we propose developing stronger connections between Part 1 and Part 2 of the schedule so that Part 1 focuses more comprehensively on the children's Internet cognition as a precursor to their cyber-safety awareness. Internet cognition needs to be understood more fully than we explored in the piloting as the *children's practices with technologies as tools*, and not just 'technologies as tools'. Cyber-safety considerations should also connect more strongly with children's existing practices and experiences with technologies and using the Internet, instead of being too abstracted to the narrative scenarios. Chaiklin (2004) argues that 'practice' should be the focus of socioculturally grounded research. He argues: 'practice is reflected in a historically developed tradition of action that grows up around producing products that satisfy a generalised need (in relation to reproduction for conditions of life)' (233–234). Our initial focus on technologies and apps as tools did not enable enough consideration of the practices that children associate with using the Internet. This included the objects and products (e.g. an iPad) that foster participation in their online activity as a social action. By expanding our sociocultural theoretical foundations to include the concept of 'practice', our goal is to achieve greater insight into children's Internet cognition from a practice- and contextually based perspective, and the relationship of this cognition to their cyber-safety awareness.

Conclusion

Children's increased access to Internet-enabled touch screen technologies predicates the need for increased understanding of young children's Internet cognition. We believe children's Internet cognition can inform the provision of cyber-safety education in early childhood. This could enable educators to develop approaches to cyber-safety education that are age-related and pedagogically appropriate for young children instead of adapting approaches intended for older children. The interview schedule we piloted is our attempt to begin thinking about children's Internet cognition and consequent cyber-safety awareness. The schedule is informed by sociocultural theory, existing research into children's understandings of the Internet and cyber-safety, and knowledge of appropriate research methods for working with young children. While the schedule shows potential for eliciting children's Internet cognition and cyber-safety awareness, further work is now needed to ensure the schedule allows opportunities for children to explain their practice-based understandings of the Internet.

Disclosure statement

No potential conflict of interest was reported by the authors.

Funding

This work was supported by the auDA Foundation; Australian Catholic University Research Fund.

ORCID

Susan Edwards http://orcid.org/0000-0002-5945-0597
Andrea Nolan http://orcid.org/0000-0003-3519-6317
Michael Henderson http://orcid.org/0000-0002-6389-8300
Helen Skouteris http://orcid.org/0000-0001-9959-5750

References

Alderson, P. 2005. "Designing Ethical Research with Children." In *Ethical Research with Children*, edited by A. Farrell, 27–37. Maidenhead: McGraw Hill.
Australian Curriculum and Assessment Reporting Authority 2014. *Australian Curriculum Foundation to Year 10, Digital Technologies Processes and Production Skills*. Accessed October 13, 2015. http://www.australiancurriculum.edu.au/technologies/digital-technologies/curriculum/f-10?layout=2&y=F-2&s=DIKU&s=DIPPS
Australian Early Development Census 2015. Accessed October 10, 2015. https://www.aedc.gov.au/
Australian Government & Australian Communications and Media Authority 2015. *Zippep's Astro Circus Lesson Plans*. Accessed July 23, 2015. https://www.esafety.gov.au/education-resources/classroom-resources/zippeps-astro-circus

Chaiklin, S. 2004. "The Role of Practice in Cultural-historical Science." In *Children, Development and Education. Cultural, Historical, Anthropological Perspectives*, edited by M. Kontopodis, C. Wulf, and B. Fichtner, 227–247. Dorchedt: Springer.

Commissioner Commonwealth of Australia 2015. *Office of the Children's ESafety*. Accessed October 13, 2015. https://www.esafety.gov.au/

Crystal, D. 2001. *Language and the Internet*. Cambridge: Cambridge University Press.

Daniels, H. 2008. *Vygotsky and Research*. New York: Routledge.

DfE (Department for Education) 2014. *Statutory Framework for the Early Years Foundation Stage*. DFE-00337-2014. http://www.gov.uk/government/publications.

DEEWR (Department of Education, Employment and Workplace) 2009. *Belonging, Being & Becoming: The Early Years Learning Framework for Australia*. Canberra: Commonwealth of Australia.

Dockett, S., J. Einarsdottir, and B. Perry. 2011. "Balancing Methodologies and Methods in Researching with Young Children." In *Researching Young Children's Perspectives: Debating the Ethics and Dilemmas of Educational Research with Children*, edited by D. Harcourt, B. Perry, and T. Waller, 68–81. Oxon: Routledge.

Dodge, A., N. Husain, and N. Duke. 2011. "Connected Kids? K-2 Children's Use and Understanding of the Internet." *Language Arts* 89 (2): 86–98.

Edwards, S., H. Skouteris, A. Nolan, and M. Henderson. 2015. "Young Children's Internet Cognition." In *Understanding Digital Technologies and Young Children: An International Perspective*, edited by S. Garvis and N. Lemon, 38–46. New York: Routledge.

Ey, L., and C. Cupit. 2011. "Exploring Young Children's Understanding of Risks Associated with Internet Usage and Their Concepts of Management Strategies." *Journal of Early Childhood Research* 9 (1): 53–65.

Fargas-Malet, M., D. McSherry, E. Larkin, and C. Robinson. 2010. "Research with Children: Methodological Issues and Innovative Techniques." *Journal of Early Childhood Research* 8 (2): 175–192.

FBI-SOS n.d. Accessed December 4, 2015. https://www.fbi.gov/news/stories/2012/october/new-cyber-safety-website-for-teachers-students

Fleer, M. 2013. "Digital Positioning for Inclusive Practice in Early Childhood: The Cultural Practices Surrounding Digital Tablets in Family Homes." *Computers in New Zealand Schools: Learning, Teaching, Technology* 25 (1–3): 56–76.

Fleer, M., and T. Hardy. 1993. "How Can We Find out What 3 and 4 Years Old Think? New Approaches to Eliciting Very Young Children's Understandings in Science." *Research in Science* 23: 68–77.

Freeman, M. 2009. "Children Rights as Human Rights: Reading the UNCRC." In *The Palgrave Handbook of Childhood Studies*, edited by J. Qvortrup, W. Corsaro, and M. S. Honig, 377–394. New York: Palgrave Macmillan.

Giant, N. 2013. *E-safety for the I-generation. Combating the Misuse and Abuse of Technology in Schools*. London: Jessica Kingsley.

Gold, J. 2015. *Screen-smart Parenting. How to Find Balance and Benefit in Your Child's Use of Social Media, Apps and Digital Devices*. New York: Guildford Press.

Greenfield, P., and Z. Yan. 2006. "Children, Adolescents, and the Internet: A New Field of Inquiry in Developmental Psychology." *Developmental Psychology* 42 (3): 391–394.

Grey, A. 2011. "Cyber-safety in Early Childhood Education." *Australasian Journal of Early Childhood* 36 (2): 77–81.

Groundwater-Smith, S., S. Dockett, and D. Bottrell. 2015. *Participatory Research with Children and Young People*. London: Sage.

Hart, R. 2008. "Stepping Back from the Ladder." In *Participation and Learning. Perspectives on Education and the Environment, Health and Sustainability*, edited by A. Reid, B. B. Jensen, J. Nikel, and V. Simovska, 19–31. Dorchedt: Springer.

Heider, K. 2015. "Cybersafety in Early Childhood: What Parents and Educators Need to Now." In *Young Children and Families in the Information Age*, edited by K. Heider and M. Jalongo, 277–292. Dorchedt: Springer.

Holloway, D., L. Green, and S. Livingstone. 2013. *Zero to Eight. Young Children and Their Internet Use*. London: EU Kids Online.

Holloway, D., L. Green, and K. Stevenson. 2015. "Digitods: Toddlers, Touchscreens and Australian Family Life." *M/C Journal* 18 (5): 1–7.

Johnson, J. 2014. "Play Provision and Pedagogy in Curricular Approaches." In *SAGE International Handbook on Play and Learning in Early Childhood*, edited by L. Brooker, B. Blaise, and S. Edwards, 180–191. Sage: London.

Joint Select Committee on Cyber-Safety 2011. *High Wire Act. Cyber-safety and the Young*. The Parliament of the Commonwealth of Australia. Accessed October 12, 2015. http://www.aph.gov.au/parliamentary_business/committees/house_of_representatives_committees?url=jscc/report.htm

Langston, A., L. Abbott, V. Lewis, and M. Kellett. 2004. "Early Childhood." In *Doing Research with Children and Young People*, edited by E. Fraser, V. Lewis, S. Ding, M. Kellett, and C. Robinson, 147–161. London: Open University Press.

Lindsay, D., M. de Zwart, M. Henderson, and M. Phillips. 2011. "Understanding Legal Risks Facing Children and Young People Using Social Network Sites." *Telecommunications Journal of Australia* 61 (1): 1–18.

Livingstone, S., L. Haddon, and A. Görzig, eds. 2012. *Children, Risk and Safety on the Internet: Research and Policy Challenges in Comparative Perspective*. Bristol: Policy Press.

Livingstone, S., G. Mascheroni, M. Dreier, S. Chaudron, and K. Lagae. 2015. *How Parents of Young Children Manage Digital Devices at Home: The Role of Income, Education and Parental Style*. London: EU Kids Online.

NAEYC (National Association for the Education of Young Children and the Fred Rogers Centre for Early Learning and Children's Media) 2012. *Technology and Interactive Media as Tools in Early Childhood Programs Serving Children from Birth through Age 8. Position Statement*. Washington, DC: NAEYC.

Nolan, A., K. Macfarlane, and J. Cartmel. 2013. *Research in Early Childhood*. London: Sage.

O'Keeffe, G., and K. Clarke-Pearson. 2011. Clinical Report. the Impact of Social Media on Children, Adolescents, and Family. *Pediatrics* 127: 800–804. doi: 10.1542/peds.2011-0054.

Plowman, L., and J. McPake. 2013. "Seven Myths about Young Children and Technology." *Childhood Education* 89 (1): 27–33.

Plowman, L., J. McPake, and C. Stephen. 2008. "Just Picking It up? Young Children Learning with Technology at Home." *Cambridge Journal of Education* 38 (3): 303–319.

Plowman, L., J. McPake, and C. Stephen. 2010. "The Technologisation of Childhood? Young Children and Technology in the Home." *Children & Society* 24 (1): 63–74. doi:10.1111/j.1099-0860.2008.00180.x.

Punch, S. 2002. Research with Children: The Same or Different from Research with Adults? *Childhood: A Journal of Global Child Research* 9 (3), 321–341.

Robbins, J. 2005. "Contexts, Collaboration, and Cultural Tools: A Sociocultural Perspective on Researching Children's Thinking." *Contemporary Issues in Early Childhood* 6 (2): 140–149.

Saracho, O. 2015. "Developmentally Appropriate Technology and Interactive Media in Early Childhood." In *Young Children and Families in the Information Age. Applications of Technology in Early Childhood*, edited by K. Heider and M. Jalongo, 183–207. Dordrecht: Springer.

Spink, A., S. Danby, K. Mallan, and C. Butler. 2010. "Exploring Young Children's Web Searching and Technoliteracy." *Journal of Documentation* 66 (2): 191–206.

Stetsenko, A. 2011. "Darwin and Vygotsky on Development: An Exegesis on Human Nature." In *Children, Development and Education. Cultural, Historical and Anthropological Perspectives*, edited by M. Kontopodis, C. Wulf, and B. Fichtner, 25–41. Dordrecht: Springer.

ThinkUKnow Corporate Report [2014] 2015. Accessed September 18, 2015. www.thinkuknow.org.au

United Kingdom Safer Internet Centre 2013. Accessed December 4, 2015. http://www.saferinternet.org.uk/

United Nations Convention on the Rights of the Child 1989. *Office of the United Nations High Commissioner for Human Rights*. Article 12.

Verenikina, I., and L. Kervin. 2011. "IPads, Digital Play and Preschoolers." *He Kupu* 2 (5): 4–19.

Vygotsky, L. S. 1997. "The History of the Development of Higher Mental Functions." In *The Collected Works of L.S. Vygotsky*. Vol. 4, edited by R. W. Rieber, 1–251. New York: Plenum Press.

Yan, Z. 2005. "Age Differences in Children's Understanding of the Complexitiy of the Internet." *Journal of Applied Developmental Psychology* 26: 385–396.

Yan, Z. 2009. "Limited Knowledge and Limited Resources: Children's and Adolescents' Understanding of the Internet." *Journal of Applied Developmental Psychology* 30: 103–115.

Index

Note: page numbers in Bold refer 'tables', italics refer 'figures'; locators followed by 'n' indicate notes section.

AAP *see* American Academy of Pediatrics (AAP)
AEDC *see* Australian Early Development Census (AEDC)
Alderson, P. 105
American Academy of Pediatrics (AAP) 6, 69
Analysing Children's Creative Thinking framework 23
AR Flashcards App 26–7, **27**
Arnott, Lorna 3
attitude theory 86
attribution theory 86
Aubrey, C. 71, 78
Australian Early Development Census (AEDC) 109
Australian Early Years Learning Framework 104

Baek, Y-M. 8
Bandura, A. 7, 15
Belk, Russell 40
Bem, D. J. 86
Bennett, M. 72, 78
BERA Ethical Guidelines 23
Bernstein, B. 62
Bird, J. 24
Bishop, J. C. 24
Broadhead, P. 24, 51, 57
Bronfenbrenner, U. 7, 15, 55
Brooker, L. 50
Brown, S. 63

Caillois, R. 23
CBeebies Playtime app 28
Chaiklin, S. 110
'circuit of culture' 33
Code of Ethics 35
communication play **25**
contemporary technologies 3
creative play **25**
Cupit, C. 104
Curtis, M. 24
cyber-safety education 4; children's understandings of 102–5; development of 106; interview schedule 106, **107–8**; lessons learned and implications for 109–11; overview of 100–2; pilot testing 109; researching with young children, methods for 105–6
'*Cyber-smart for young kids*' 105

Dahl, S. 71, 78
deep play **25**, 27
Deutsche Gesellschaft für Erziehungswissenschaft (DGfE) 35
Digital Consumerist Context 51
digital literacy 39–40
Digital Play Framework 24, 49–50
Digital Play System 55–6, *56*, 58–9, 63
Dodge, A. 103
dramatic play **25**
Duke, N. 103
Dunkels, Elza 3

early childhood education (ECE) 83; attribution and attitude theory 86; digital devices 83–4, 86, **95**; digital-play pedagogical practices 84–5; factors affecting digital technologies in 85–6; focus groups 90; online survey 87–8; play-based pedagogy 84–5, 89, **90**, 95–6; qualitative outcomes 90–3; quantitative outcomes 88–90, **89**, **90**
Early Years Foundation Stage 104
ECE *see* early childhood education (ECE)
ecological exploration: affordances of technologies 60–2, *61*; children and practitioners 63; children's social participation 57, 63–4; Contextualist perspective 52; data collection 52–3;

Digital Play System 55–6, *56*, 58–9, **59**; digital technologies 50–2; Matrix of Social Status Roles 57–8; overview of 49–50; Preschool System 59–60, *60*; reciprocal behaviours and interactions 57; systems, routines and practices 62; technological positions 58; technologies observed in preschools **53**; theoretical guide 55
ecological systems theory 55
educational contexts, digital media usage in 33
Edwards, S. 22, 24, 70, 85
Emilia, Reggio 50
epistemic play 23
Estonian parents, attitudes and practices of: bio-ecological framework 7; data analysis 11; data collection 9–10; digital play practices 8, 12–14; digital technology and smart devices 5; parental mediation 9, 14–15; respondents 10–111; smart devices usage, infants and toddlers 11–12; social cognitive theory 7
exploratory play **25**
'exploring play and creativity in preschool children's use of apps' project 22–3
Ey, L. 104

Falloon, G. 70
fantasy play **25**
FBI-SOS online programme 105
FLH technique *see* Fundamental Lexical Hypothesis (FLH) technique
focal-technology approach 53
Folkesson, A. -M. 69, 78
Frey, D. 86
Fundamental Lexical Hypothesis (FLH) technique 87–8

Gee, J. P. 71, 78
Goffman, Erving 41
Goodwin, K. 8, 11, **13**, 15
Google Forms 9
Greenfield, P. 102
Grey, A. 104

Hart, R. 105
Heider, K. 104
Highfield, K. 8, 11
High Wire Act 105
Howard, J. 69, 71, 77–8
Hughes, B. 28; definition, for play types **25**, 27–8; taxonomy of play 20, 24
Husain, N. 103
Hutt, C. 23, 24

imaginative play **25**, 26
internet cognition 4, 101–2; children's understandings of 102–5, **103**; development of 106; interview schedule 106, **107–8**; lessons learned and implications for 109–11; pilot testing 109; researching with young children, methods for 105–6

Jahnke, I. 76
Janks, H. 78, 79
Jansz, J. 16

Kalaš, I 1
Karila, K. 69, 71
Katz, D. 86
Kim, K. -S. 8
kindergarten class, as social world 3; apparent ease of integration 41–2, *42*; children's own efforts *37*; children use digital technology 32; 'circuit of culture' 33; classroom activities *36*; mediatization process 33–4; online tools 34; Padlet wall *36*; parents perspective 43–5; procedures in 35; public visibility 42–3; selection process 34; semi-standardized interviews 34–5; teacher's perspective *see* teacher's perspective, in kindergarten; Twitter, in class meeting *37*, 38
Knauf, Helen 3
Kozinets, R. V. 72
Kumar, S. 76

Lafton, T. 68, 69, 79
Lantz-Andersson, A. 78, 79
Lauricella, A. 15
Lee, J. -M. 8
Levin, T. 85
Lindahl, M. G. 69, 78
Ljung-Djärf, A. 58, 68, 69, 73, 76, 77, 79
locomotor play **25**
ludic play 23
Lynch, J. 69, 70

McPake, J. 94
Marklund, L. 3, 78
Marsh, Jackie 3
mastery play **25**
Matrix of Social Status Roles 57–8
Merchant, G. 70, 71
Miles, G. E. 69, 71, 77–8
Miller, Daniel 43
Minecraft app 26, **26**, 28

National Association for the Education of Young Children (NAEYC) 105
Nevski, Elyna 3
Nikken, P. 16

object play **25**
Office of the Children's eSafety Commissioner 105

Organisation for Economic Co-operation and Development (OECD) 68
Østerud, S. 69, 70, 72, 78, 79

Palmér, H. 70, 78
parental mediation, during child's digital play 9, 14–15
Parise, M. 72, 78
Parten, M. B. 51
play-based pedagogy 51, 52, 84–5, 89, **90**, 91, 95–6
Plowman, L. 8, 94
Positive Online Content and Services for Children in Europe (POSCON) 13
Pramling, P. 79
Preschool System 59–60, *60*, 62, 64

Rantavuori, L. 69
recapitulative play **25**, 28
Redpath, T. 69, 70
Rees-Davies, L. 69, 71, 77–8
Rideout, V. J. 15, 21
Robson, S. 23
role play **25**
rough play **25**, 28

SAMR model *see* Substitution, Augmentation, Modification and Redefinition (SAMR) model
Samuelsson, U. 78
Sandvik, M. 69, 70, 72, 78, 79
Schachter, S. 86
science, technology, engineering and maths (STEM) 51
Scottish Educational Research Association (SERA) 52
screen-based technologies 2
semi-standardized interviews 34–5
SERA *see* Scottish Educational Research Association (SERA)
Siibak, Andra 3
Siraj-Blatchford, J. 50
Skantz Åberg, E. 79
Smørdal, O. 69, 70, 72, 78, 79
social cognitive theory 7
social participation framework 51
social play **25**
Social Play Continuum 24, 51, 57
sociocultural theory 102
socio-dramatic play **25**
Stahlberg, D. 86
STEM *see* science, technology, engineering and maths (STEM)
Stephen, C. 8, 63
Substitution, Augmentation, Modification and Redefinition (SAMR) model 39
Swedish preschool teachers: analysis 73–4; caring rationality 74–5; ethical considerations 73; individual knowledge 71–2; literacy, definition of 67; materiality 70–1; materials 72; nurturing 75–6; online ethnographic method 72; participants 73; procedure 72; risk discourse 68–9; teaching rationality 76
Swedish Scientific Council 73
symbolic play **25**

Talking Tom app 27
Taylor, R. 26
teacher's perspective, in kindergarten: changing intentions 38–9; digital literacy 39–40; involving parents 40; professional development 40–1
Technological Pedagogical Content Knowledge framework 73
Temple Run App 27, **27**
tool mediation, for young children 102
transgressive play 27–8
tumble play **25**, 28
Twitter, in class meeting *37*, 38

UK Safer Internet Centre 105
UNESCO 1
United Nations Convention on the Rights of the Child 105

Vandewater, E. A. 21
Vygotsky, L. 22

Wadmany, R. 85
Wartella, E. 15, 21
Weiner, B. 86

Yan, Z. 102–3
Yelland, N. J. 6, 18